PAYCHECK FINANCIAL FREEDOM

Melanie Newell

Copyright © 2024 Paycheck to Financial Freedom by Melanie Newell. All rights reserved.

The content of this book, or any part of it, cannot be replicated or utilized without the publisher's or author's explicit written consent. The only exception to this rule is using short quotes for a book review.

This book is designed to provide accurate and authoritative information regarding personal finance. It is sold with the understanding that neither the author nor the publisher is engaged in rendering financial, investment, legal, accounting, or other professional services.

While the publisher and author have used their best efforts in preparing this book, they make no representations or warranties concerning the accuracy or completeness of the book's contents and expressly disclaim any implied warranties of merchantability or fitness for a particular purpose.

The advice and strategies contained herein may not be suitable for your situation. You should do extensive research or consult with a professional when appropriate. Neither the publisher nor the author shall be liable for any loss of profit or other commercial damages, including but not limited to special, incidental, consequential, personal, or other damages.

Listen to *Paycheck to Financial Freedom* on **Audible.com**.

Contents

INTRODUCTION 7

ROOT CAUSES 11

Reasons for Financial Struggle 11

Exercise: Root Causes 16

FINANCIAL LITERACY QUICK START 17

Financial Education 17

Money Fundamentals 20

Exercise: Financial Literacy 102 30

BUDGET YOUR WAY TO FREEDOM 33

Budgeting 33

Budgeting Methods 35

Goal Setting 37

Exercise: Your Budget 41

MINDING YOUR MEANS 45

Causes and Solutions 45

Needs Versus Wants 52

Exercise: Live Within Your Means 54

HIGH COSTS: MANHATTAN 55
Cost of Living Factors 55
Reducing Costs 57
Exercise: Reduce Living Costs 62

THE DEBT TERMINATOR 63
Debt Fundamentals 63
Compounding Interest 67
Effective Debt Management 68
Debt Elimination Strategies 70
Mortgage Debt 73
Exercise: Kick Debt Butt 75

MORE MONEY, FEWER PROBLEMS 77
Increase Your Income 77
Beware of Scams 86
Exercise: Income Boost 90

RAINY DAYS, SUNNY TOMORROWS 91
Emergency Funds for Rainy Days 91
Pay Day Loans 93
Savings for Sunny Tomorrows 95

Exercise: Stress Testing	97
30+ TOP MONEY-SAVING TIPS	**98**
General Tips	98
Grocery and Household Tips	101
Clothing Tips	105
Banking Tips	105
Other Tips	106
MONEY MINDSET MAKEOVER	**111**
Mind Over Money	111
Transformation and Growth	116
Family Engagement	122
FIVE-STAR FINANCIAL APPS	**125**
Education	125
Budgeting	126
Debt Reduction	127
Credit Scores	127
Mobile Banking	129
Mortgage Rates	129
Investing	130

Money Transfer (Local) — 131

Money Transfer (International) — 132

Tax Preparation — 133

Coupon Sites — 134

Cost of Living Calculators — 135

FROM PAYCHECK TO PROSPERITY — 137

INTRODUCTION

I was $114,000 in debt and living from paycheck to paycheck with little hope. One day, I said, "Enough is enough," it was time to solve my financial frustration. My monthly earnings were decent, so income wasn't the problem. Instead, my financial insecurity was due to a lack of financial literacy, planning, and self-accountability.

I began learning money management basics, changing my habits, and budgeting. Months later, I broke my paycheck-to-paycheck struggles and reduced my debt significantly. Now, I'm in control of my financial life and debt-free. I want the same joy and power to enter your life.

Welcome to *Paycheck to Financial Freedom*, a transformative guide crafted to illuminate a path toward financial abundance and fulfillment. In a world often dominated by the ebb and flow of paychecks, this book is your compass, leading you beyond financial constraints toward a prosperous future.

Many find themselves caught in the tide of paycheck-to-paycheck living, where financial stress and uncertainty become constant companions. Financial problems can be overwhelming and can affect every aspect of our lives. They can cause stress, anxiety, and even depression. But the truth is that most financial problems have a root cause that can be identified and addressed. In writing this book, I aim to help you identify those root causes and provide practical solutions to overcome them.

This book is not just about budgeting or saving; it's a holistic exploration of the myriad factors influencing your financial journey. Each chapter is a stepping stone toward a more prosperous life, from unraveling the root causes of financial struggles to embracing financial literacy, budgeting, and fostering a positive mindset.

The transition from paycheck-centric thinking to a wealth mindset involves practical financial strategies and a shift in perspective. It's about recognizing the abundance of opportunities, cultivating healthy financial habits, and unleashing your potential to create a life where financial worries no longer dominate your thoughts.

In the following chapters, we'll delve into the complexities of personal finance, exploring strategies to break free from paycheck doom and gloom cycles. From practical budgeting techniques to fostering a positive financial mindset, each chapter is designed to empower you with the knowledge and tools needed to redefine your relationship with money.

I understand that personal finance can seem daunting, and I promise to present the material in a way that is easy to understand and accessible to anyone. I'll share examples and real-world applications to help illustrate the concepts and strategies discussed.

I hope that by reading this book, you will gain a deeper understanding of personal finance and feel empowered to take control of your financial future. Whether you are just starting out or already well on your way, I believe the principles and techniques discussed in these pages can help you achieve your financial dreams and create a brighter future for yourself and your loved ones.

Are you ready to embark on this journey? *Paycheck to Financial Freedom* is not just a book; it's an invitation to reimagine your financial future, break free from limitations, and embrace a life where prosperity is not just a distant dream but a tangible reality. Let the journey begin.

How to Navigate This Book

Navigating this book is meant to be a personal expedition, and I encourage you to embrace it at your own pace. Each chapter is a self-contained module that delves into specific financial matters. While this book was written with American consumers in mind, financial concepts are global. Therefore, this book will help you regardless of where you're based. You must only seek the equivalent resources in your country.

Take the time to absorb the insights, engage with the exercises, and reflect on the principles presented. Treat each chapter as a building block, gradually constructing a robust foundation for your financial future.

By the end of the book, you'll understand the reasons for your financial pitfalls and the steps you can take to rectify them. Then, you can create a custom plan to improve your financial circumstances and security within a suitable timeframe. Finally, you'll build a better relationship with money to improve your well-being and peace of mind.

Chapter 1
ROOT CAUSES

Why are you living paycheck to paycheck? Why have you amassed considerable debt? Why don't you have savings? You may have thought about these questions but could not pinpoint the exact reasons.

To make financial progress, you must understand your financial predicament's underlying reason or reasons. This will invite greater self-awareness behind your money management habits and move you closer to finding solutions. Let's review several potential causes of ongoing financial instability in this chapter.

Reasons for Financial Struggle

Low Financial Literacy

Are you among the millions who didn't receive a financial education from your parents or school? Don't worry, you're not alone. However, low financial literacy can significantly contribute to the cycle of living paycheck to paycheck, trapping individuals in a precarious economic situation.

Financial literacy refers to the understanding and knowledge of various financial aspects, including budgeting, saving, investing, and debt management. When individuals lack this essential knowledge, they may make uninformed decisions that hinder their financial stability. For instance, financial literacy directs people to create and adhere to a budget. Without understanding that, individuals may struggle to manage their income effectively. For example, they might overspend on non-essential items, leaving little or no money for essential expenses like rent, utilities, and groceries.

Improving financial literacy is essential for breaking the cycle of living paycheck to paycheck, eradicating debt, and saving money. Education and resources that promote understanding of personal finance can empower individuals to make informed decisions, build financial resilience, and work towards long-term economic well-being.

Lack of Financial Discipline

I've met many people who are financially literate but lack the discipline to manage their money efficiently. However, discipline is crucial for making informed decisions, sticking to a budget, and cultivating responsible financial habits.

When individuals lack discipline in managing their money, they are more likely to spend impulsively, neglect savings, and accumulate debt. For example, Joe goes to the grocery store with a list but purchases unnecessary items.

Developing financial discipline and excellent habits enables individuals to regain control of their finances instead of being careless when it matters most.

No Financial Goals

Having no financial goals can contribute significantly to financial struggle, as it often reflects a lack of direction and purpose in managing one's finances. It's the equivalent of blowing in the wind and hoping to end up somewhere promising.

Financial goals provide a roadmap for individuals to plan, save, and invest wisely, helping them achieve stability and build wealth over time. For instance, financial objectives motivate one to save money for specific purposes, such as buying a home, starting a business, or funding education. Without clear objectives, individuals may lack the incentive to save, leading to a lack of emergency funds and an increased reliance on credit in times of need.

Establishing financial targets is crucial for creating a path and future for managing one's finances. Goals motivate you to make informed decisions, prioritize spending, save consistently, and work towards a more secure financial future. By setting and regularly reviewing financial objectives, individuals can break free from paycheck stress cycles and build a foundation for financial success.

Live Beyond Your Means

Spending more than you earn is a fundamental financial mistake that can quickly lead to a routine of living paycheck to paycheck. When expenses consistently exceed income, individuals find themselves in precarious financial situations, struggling to cover necessities and often relying on each paycheck to meet immediate needs. For example, living beyond one's means restricts financial flexibility. Adapting to changes in income, unexpected expenses, or economic downturns becomes challenging. This lack of flexibility makes it difficult to break the cycle of relying solely on each paycheck to meet financial obligations.

Breaking the cycle of living paycheck to paycheck often starts with addressing overspending. This may involve creating a realistic budget, prioritizing needs over wants, identifying areas for cost-cutting, and developing healthy financial behaviors. By living within one's means, individuals can regain control of their finances, build savings, and achieve more economic stability and peace of mind.

It's worth noting that even wealthy people can overspend and face difficulties with weekly money management. So, regardless of your net worth, spending that outpaces earnings will lead to shortfalls.

High Living Costs

Hawaii, California, and Massachusetts are frequently in the top five of the most expensive states, and many Californian cities rank in the top 25. Then, there are global rankings, which may include your current location.

The cost of living, including housing, utilities, healthcare, and education, can be high in certain regions. Rising expenses and inflation can quickly outpace income, leaving little room for savings or emergency funds.

High living expenses can significantly contribute to paycheck shortfalls, creating a situation where individuals struggle to cover their costs despite receiving regular income. When living costs exceed one's earnings, it can lead to financial stress and a constant struggle to cover expenses.

Consumer Debt

Consumer debt can significantly contribute to paycheck-to-paycheck stress, as it adds a financial burden that individuals must carry monthly. When consumer debt, such as credit card balances or personal loans, accumulates, it can result in a substantial portion of income being dedicated to debt repayment, leaving little room for saving or covering other essential expenses. For example, high-interest rates can make it challenging to get ahead financially, forcing individuals to allocate a significant portion of their income toward debt servicing. Alternatively, paying only the minimum amount due on consumer debts can lead to a prolonged repayment period. The minimum payments, while providing temporary relief, often strain monthly budgets, leaving individuals with limited funds for other things.

Insufficient Income

Insufficient income is a primary and straightforward factor commonly associated with weekly paycheck shortages. When an individual's earnings are not enough to cover essential expenses, including housing, utilities, food, and other basic needs, they often find themselves in a constant struggle to make ends meet. For example, low-income earners often find it challenging to build an emergency fund. They may be forced to rely on credit cards or loans to cover unexpected expenses, further exacerbating their financial obstacles.

Addressing the challenges of living paycheck to paycheck due to insufficient income often requires a multifaceted approach. We'll cover ways to boost your income later.

No Emergency Fund

I recently read a news headline that stated roughly two in three Americans can't cover a $500 emergency. Yet, we know life is full of surprises in the way of unplanned events. So, there's a disconnect here.

Unforeseen emergencies, such as medical bills, car repairs, home maintenance, and family issues, can strain finances. Individuals may use credit or cut back on other necessities without an emergency fund to cover these unexpected costs.

Establishing an emergency fund provides a safety net, reduces reliance on credit, and enhances overall financial resilience, helping individuals better navigate financial challenges and avoid paycheck shortfalls.

Lack of Savings

Savings serve as a financial cushion, providing a buffer against unexpected expenses, emergencies, and fluctuations in income. Individuals with inadequate or no savings may struggle to navigate financial challenges.

To break free from the cycle of paycheck shortfalls due to a lack of savings, one should set aside a portion of income for savings, for example, $25 monthly, to build cash reserves.

Social and Peer Pressure

Social and peer pressure can contribute to paycheck-to-paycheck living by influencing individuals to conform to certain spending norms, engage in random purchases, or prioritize short-term gratification over long-term financial stability. The desire to fit in, maintain a particular lifestyle, or meet societal expectations can lead individuals to make financial decisions that may strain their budgets and perpetuate weekly paycheck frustration. For instance, Susy attends brunch weekly with old college friends at a pricey restaurant. While she understands the importance of maintaining friendships and networking, the cost of brunch weighs on her finances.

Exercise: Root Causes

I want you to actively participate in changing your fortunes, and you'll do that by reflecting on and applying information in this book.

Your first assignment is to consider the root causes above and those that apply to you. You can also prioritize them or give them weightings to understand the most problematic ones. The following is an example.

Bill's Reasons for Struggling Financially

1. Lack of financial discipline
2. No emergency fund or savings
3. Consumer debt (mainly student debt)

Only when you understand your underlying challenges can you seek to solve each matter. Moreover, you'll gain insights and answers throughout this book to help you transition from paycheck to financial freedom.

Chapter 2
Financial Literacy Quick Start

Congratulations! You're improving and investing in your financial literacy by reading this book. That's vital and something you should do regularly because there's no escaping financial matters. Instead, a person depends on economics and financial resources to survive. So, it can be said that each life is a financial life to some extent.

Financial literacy prepares you to navigate said financial life for the better. It gives you the knowledge and tools to optimize finances, achieve financial security, and gain peace of mind.

Let's review several fundamental financial concepts that will support better money management. Some of these concepts will be new, while others will be a review.

Financial Education

Financial education is available to anyone who wants it, and 99% of the time, it's free. Visit countless websites, blogs, YouTube channels, and social media feeds for a steady diet of information and advice.

Online courses are plentiful and suitable for people who want more structure. Amazon carries personal finance books in three formats: e-book, hardcopy, and audiobook. Banks and financial institutions offer educational hubs, workshops, newsletters, and monthly webinars. Finally, your local library has books and programs dealing with money management. Therefore, pursuing financial literacy has more to do with a person's degree of interest than the availability of materials.

What topics should you grasp? While the goal isn't necessarily to become a financial expert, you'll want a conversational understanding of daily cash management, budgeting, debt, credit, savings, investing, and retirement planning. More knowledge might include financial planning, insurance, taxes, and estate planning.

Choosing reputable financial educators is crucial for acquiring accurate and valuable information about managing money. Here are vital factors to consider when selecting financial educators:

Look for educators with relevant qualifications, such as degrees in finance, economics, or certifications in financial planning. Consider their professional experience and expertise in the field of personal finance.

Check if reputable industry organizations or associations recognize the financial educator. Look for affiliations with well-known financial institutions, educational institutions, or professional groups.

Explore reviews on online platforms, social media, or their website to gauge the satisfaction of past participants. Seek feedback from previous clients or attendees of their workshops or courses.

Assess the educator's commitment to transparency and ethical standards.

Ensure they adhere to a code of ethics and conflicts of interest do not influence their financial advice.

Evaluate the content of their educational materials or courses to ensure they cover practical and applicable financial concepts. Look for educators who focus on real-world scenarios and provide actionable advice.

Consider the educator's teaching style and whether it aligns with your preferred learning approach. Some educators may use interactive methods, case studies, or real-life examples to enhance the learning experience.

Ensure the financial educator provides supplementary resources, such as articles, guides, or tools, to support ongoing learning. Ensure that the resources are easily accessible and user-friendly.

Assess the educator's ability to communicate complex financial concepts clearly and engagingly. Look for educators encouraging interaction, questions, and discussions during their sessions.

Financial information and regulations change, so choose educators who stay current with industry trends and updates.

Check for recent publications, blog posts, or other ongoing learning and professional development indicators.

Consider the cost of the educational program or services relative to the value provided. Evaluate whether the investment in financial education aligns with the quality and depth of the content offered.

Look for educators who prioritize inclusivity and cater to diverse audiences.

Check if the financial educator offers a refund policy or satisfaction guarantee, indicating their confidence in the value of their educational offerings.

Start your journey with the following resources:

- The Balance covers personal finance with articles and guides on budgeting, investing, taxes, and other financial activities.
- Investopedia is a comprehensive financial education website with articles, tutorials, and educational content covering various financial topics, from investing to economics.
- NerdWallet offers comprehensive guides, calculators, and articles on various personal finance topics, including credit cards, banking, investing, and insurance.
- Known for its investment advice and stock market insights, The Motley Fool provides educational resources on personal finance, investing, and retirement planning.
- The Vanguard Group, or Vanguard, is one of the largest investment management companies globally. Visit their resources and education pages for trustworthy advice.

Those are five websites in a landscape of many. So, if you didn't find any of them appealing, no problem. Educators and content come in all shapes and sizes. So, it might take time to find a match. It's kind of like dating. Secondly, unlike studying medicine or law, personal finance sees fewer new developments. So, once you build a robust foundation, you'll seek additional info as your life progresses. For example, someone entering retirement may research government and income benefits.

Money Fundamentals

Goal Setting

Goal setting is a fundamental aspect of effective financial planning and relief, providing individuals with a roadmap for achieving desired outcomes and ensuring long-term financial well-being. Setting monetary goals involves establishing clear, short-term, or long-term objectives and creating a strategic plan to attain them.

Goal setting provides direction and purpose to financial decisions. It helps individuals clarify their priorities and focus on what matters most. Having specific financial objectives provides motivation and discipline. Goals create a sense of urgency and purpose, encouraging individuals to make informed and intentional decisions.

Financial ambitions should be measurable, allowing individuals to track their progress over time. This quantifiable progress is a source of encouragement and helps individuals stay on course.

Goals serve as a guide for financial decision-making. When faced with choices, individuals can evaluate options based on whether they align with their established goals. Achieving financial objectives contributes to a sense of accomplishment and improved financial wellness. It provides a foundation for economic stability and security.

Short-term goals typically have a timeframe of one year or less. They can include building an emergency fund, paying off a small debt, or saving for a vacation.

Long-term goals have a timeframe of several years or more. Examples include buying a home, saving for a child's education, or building a retirement fund.

Specificity is critical for goal setting. For example, instead of a vague goal like "save money," specify the amount you want to save and the purpose, e.g., "save $5,000 for a down payment on a home."

Income

Income refers to the money or earnings an individual receives regularly in exchange for goods, services, or labor. It is a crucial aspect of personal finance as it is the primary source of funds for meeting various financial obligations, expenses, and goals. Income can come from multiple sources, including employment, self-employment, investments, rental properties, and business activities.

Types of income include:

Earned income is earned through active participation in work or business activities. This includes salaries, wages, bonuses, and self-employment earnings.

Passive income is generated without active involvement in day-to-day activities. Examples include rental income, investment dividends, interest from savings accounts, and book royalties.

Portfolio income derives from investments, such as capital gains, dividends, and interest from stocks, bonds, and other securities.

Business income comes from operating a business. This includes profits, earnings, and other financial gains from business activities.

Unearned income is received without direct participation in earning it. This includes gifts, inheritances, and certain government benefits like Social Security or unemployment benefits.

Gross Versus Net Income

Gross income is an individual's total earnings before deductions or taxes are subtracted. For employees, gross income includes the salary or wages agreed upon in their employment contract. For self-employed individuals, gross income encompasses total revenue before deducting business expenses.

Net income, or take-home pay or net pay, is the money an individual receives after deducting taxes and other mandatory deductions from their gross income. Employees' net income appears on their paycheck after deductions for income tax, Social Security, Medicare, and other benefits. For self-employed individuals, net income is the profit remaining after subtracting business expenses from gross revenue.

Understanding Take-Home Pay

1. Determine Gross Income: Identify the total gross income and the earnings before any deductions.
2. Deduct Federal Income Tax: Subtract the federal income tax withholding based on the individual's taxable income and tax brackets.
3. Deduct State and Local Taxes: State and local income taxes may also be deducted depending on the individual's location.
4. Subtract FICA Taxes: Deduct the FICA (Federal Insurance Contributions Act) taxes, which include Social Security and Medicare contributions.
5. Account for Other Deductions: Consider any additional deductions, such as health insurance premiums, retirement contributions, and other voluntary deductions.
6. Calculate Net Income: The result is the individual's net income, or take-home pay, representing the actual amount they receive.

Task: Review your most recent paycheck and identify deductions.

Expenses

Expenses refer to the costs or monetary outflows incurred by individuals, households, businesses, or organizations in generating income, maintaining operations, and fulfilling various needs and obligations. For most individuals, expenses are unavoidable because our basic needs require food and shelter to survive.

Expenses fall into various categories: fixed, variable, non-discretionary, discretionary, irregular, and debt. Here are some examples:

Fixed or Set Expenses:
Mortgage or Rent: Monthly payments for housing.
Utilities: Regular bills for electricity, water, gas, and other essential services.

Variable or Fluctuating Expenses:
Groceries: Spending on food and household necessities.
Transportation: Costs related to fuel, public transportation, maintenance, and repairs.

Non-Discretionary or Essential Expenses:
Basic Utilities: Essential services like water, electricity, and heating.
Healthcare: Costs related to medical services, prescriptions, and health insurance.

Discretionary or Optional Expenses:
Dining Out: Money spent on meals at restaurants or take-out.
Travel: Expenses related to vacations, flights, hotels, and sightseeing.

Irregular or Periodic Expenses:
Home Maintenance: Costs for repairs and upkeep of the home.
Car Maintenance: Expenses for routine maintenance or unexpected repairs.

Debt or Loan Payments:
Car Loan Payments: Monthly payments for auto loans.
Mortgage Payments: Monthly payments for a home loan.

Cash Management

Monthly cash management lies in balancing income and expenses. Ideally, income should exceed costs, allowing for savings and investments.

Creating a budget is essential for effective cash management. It involves listing all sources of income and categorizing expenses, allowing individuals to plan their spending and ensure that costs do not exceed income. We'll cover this later.

Regularly monitoring both income and expenses is crucial. This can be done manually, with the help of spreadsheets, or using budgeting apps and software. Tracking helps identify spending patterns, unnecessary expenses, and potential savings opportunities.

Monthly cash management is not a set-and-forget process. It requires ongoing adjustments to account for changes in income, unexpected expenses, or shifts in financial goals. Being flexible and ready to adjust the budget is critical to maintaining financial balance.

Keeping debt under control is an essential aspect of cash management. High-interest debt, such as credit card debt, can quickly eat into your income, limiting your ability to cover expenses and save.

Debt, Credit, and Loans

Most of us aren't heirs to fortunes. So, we require loans and credit to purchase things like clothes and homes.

Debt, credit, and loans are fundamental to personal finance and the broader economy. They enable individuals and businesses to invest, purchase goods and services, and manage cash flow over time. Understanding the different types of debt is essential for making informed decisions about borrowing and managing debt effectively.

Debt arises when an individual, company, or other entity borrows money and must repay the lender according to agreed-upon terms. This usually includes the repayment of the original amount borrowed (the principal) plus interest, compensating the lender for the risk of lending and the time value of money. For example, Tom borrows $5,000 at a 10% annual percentage rate or APR.

Credit refers to the ability to borrow money or access goods or services with the understanding that repayment will occur in the future. Creditworthiness, or the likelihood of repayment, is typically evaluated based on an individual's or entity's credit history, income, and other factors. Credit can come in various forms, including credit cards, lines of credit, and loans.

Loans are a type of debt where a lender provides funds to a borrower, who agrees to repay the principal amount and interest over a specified period. Loans can be used for various purposes, including purchasing a home, financing education, or funding a business venture. Prioritizing debt repayment is crucial for financial health.

Savings

Saving involves setting aside a portion of income rather than spending it immediately. For short-term needs or future aspirations, saving is a fundamental aspect of financial planning.

Savings serve as the foundation for an emergency fund, providing a financial safety net to cover unexpected expenses such as medical bills, car repairs, or job loss.

Accumulating savings contributes to overall financial security, reducing dependence on credit and mitigating the impact of unforeseen financial challenges.

Saving enables individuals to work towards specific goals, such as buying a home, funding education, taking a vacation, or retiring comfortably.

Having savings provides peace of mind, knowing that financial resources are available to handle life's uncertainties and pursue opportunities.

Savings help individuals avoid reliance on high-interest debt when faced with unexpected expenses. This reduces the financial stress associated with debt repayment.

Standard savings options include bank accounts, money market securities (treasury bills, certificates of deposit, etc.), and investments (stocks, bonds, etc.).

Net Worth

Net worth is a financial metric representing the difference between an individual's or entity's assets and liabilities. In simple terms, it is a measure of one's wealth and economic standing. To calculate net worth, you subtract total liabilities (debts and financial obligations) from total assets (everything owned with monetary value). The result can be positive, negative, or zero.

Here's the formula for calculating net worth:

Net Worth = Total Assets − Total Liabilities

Total Assets: This includes everything an individual or entity owns, such as cash, investments, real estate, vehicles, personal possessions, and other valuable items.

Total Liabilities: This comprises all debts and financial obligations, including mortgages, loans, credit card balances, and other outstanding liabilities.

A positive net worth indicates that assets exceed liabilities, reflecting financial health and wealth. Conversely, a negative net worth means that liabilities surpass assets, suggesting financial indebtedness. Net worth is a valuable metric for assessing financial progress and setting targets.

Taxes

Taxes play a crucial role in the functioning of economies and governments worldwide. They are the primary source of revenue for governments, enabling them to fund public services, infrastructure, and various programs. Understanding the basics of taxes is essential for individuals and businesses to comply with tax laws, manage their finances effectively, and make informed financial decisions.

Tax categories include income, sales, property, corporate, excise, payroll, capital gains, and estate.

Individuals must file income tax returns annually, reporting their income, deductions, and credits. They can reduce their taxable income by claiming deductions for qualified expenses and credits for specific situations, such as education or energy efficiency.

Whether your tax matters are straightforward or complicated, it pays to have competent accountants or tax advisors working on your behalf to navigate complex tax laws and ensure compliance.

Inflation

Inflation in the context of personal finance can be likened to the slow but steady rise in the cost of living over time. Imagine going to your favorite coffee shop and discovering that the price of your favorite coffee has increased. When it happens across the board for most goods and services, this price increase reflects inflation at work.

Ideally, your income should increase at least as fast as inflation. If your wage increases are below the inflation rate, you're effectively earning less over time, making it harder to keep up with the rising cost of living. Negotiating your salary or seeking higher-paying opportunities becomes crucial during high inflation.

Daily, you might need to adjust your budget to accommodate higher prices for essentials like groceries, gas, and utilities. This might mean cutting back on non-essential spending or finding ways to increase your income.

The most direct impact of inflation on personal finance is that over time, the same amount of money will buy fewer goods and services. If inflation is at 3% per year, something that costs $100 now will cost $103 a year from now. This might not seem like much at first, but over several years, the effect compounds, significantly reducing your purchasing power.

Putting money under your mattress or in a non-interest-bearing account means it will lose value in real terms over time due to inflation. If your savings don't grow at a rate that outpaces inflation, you're effectively losing money. For example, if you have $1,000 saved and inflation is 3%, you will need $1,030 next year to have the same purchasing power. If your savings don't grow by at least this amount, your money will purchase less.

When considering investing, one of your aims should be choosing investments that will grow faster than inflation. This means looking for investment opportunities that offer returns that are not just positive but higher than the inflation rate to ensure your money's purchasing power grows over time.

Insurance

Insurance offers protection against unforeseen events that could otherwise lead to significant financial setbacks, including accidents, illnesses, or property damage. Insurance provides peace of mind, knowing one is financially protected against various risks. This sense of security allows individuals to focus on their goals without constant worry about potential financial hardships.

Insurance helps protect valuable assets, such as homes, vehicles, and businesses, by covering repair or replacement costs in case of damage or loss.

Some types of insurance, like auto insurance, are legally required in many jurisdictions. The necessary coverage ensures compliance with regulations and protects individuals from legal consequences.

Common types of insurance include the following:
- Health insurance covers medical expenses, including hospital stays, surgeries, and prescription medications. It helps individuals manage the high healthcare costs and promotes regular medical check-ups and preventive care.
- Life insurance provides a financial payout to beneficiaries in the event of the insured's death. It is

insured for giving financial support to dependents, covering funeral expenses, and paying off debts.
- Disability insurance provides income replacement if an individual cannot work due to a disability. It ensures financial stability during periods of reduced or lost income.
- Long-term care insurance covers the costs associated with assisted living, nursing home care, or home healthcare for individuals who need extended care due to aging or illness.
- Homeowners insurance protects against damage to a home and its contents due to fire, theft, or natural disasters. Renters insurance covers personal belongings in a rented property.
- Auto insurance protects against financial losses from car accidents, theft, or damage. It covers liability, property damage, and medical expenses.
- Liability insurance protects against legal claims and financial losses resulting from personal responsibility for injuries or damages to others. It is common in auto and homeowners' insurance.

Exercise: Financial Literacy 102

We've covered some essential financial topics and concepts to help you better understand your financial matters. For example, understanding the difference between non-discretionary and discretionary expenses may help curtail optional spending.

In this exercise, I want you to find two financial learning resources you'll use weekly to improve your financial intelligence and discipline. It can be a website or YouTuber that appeals to you, for example, a female financial coach in her 30s on YouTube. Subscribe for new content notifications and make financial literacy an exciting part of your week.

Alternatively, you can create a learning plan outlining what you will do weekly or monthly to develop your financial literacy.

For instance, you will spend two hours reading a personal finance book weekly and complete one book monthly for three months.

Chapter 3
BUDGET YOUR WAY TO FREEDOM

Unless you know how to prepare a meal by heart, you'll follow a recipe to ensure it turns out delicious. I liken a budget to a recipe in that it guides and informs you on efficient money management. A budget also allows you to set realistic goals because you'll know where you stand with your finances monthly.

Let's explore budgeting, techniques, and goal setting in this chapter.

Budgeting

A budget is a financial plan that outlines your expected income and expenses over a specific period, typically monthly or annually. It serves as a roadmap for managing and allocating your financial resources, helping you achieve your financial desires and control your money. A well-designed budget considers regular and irregular expenses, allowing you to make informed decisions about spending and saving.

The advantages of budgeting include the following:

A budget provides a clear overview of your financial situation, allowing you to monitor and control your expenses. This control helps prevent overspending and promotes responsible financial management.

By setting specific financial targets within your budget, you can work towards achieving objectives such as saving for a vacation, paying off debt, or building an emergency fund.

Creating a budget encourages you to track and understand your expenses. This awareness helps identify unnecessary spending and areas where you can cut back, ultimately saving money.

A budget enables you to allocate funds for debt repayment. It helps prioritize high-interest debts and systematically reduce or eliminate them, improving financial health.

Budgeting allows you to allocate some of your income to savings and investments. Whether saving for short-term goals like a new gadget or long-term goals like retirement, a budget ensures intentional saving.

Building an emergency fund is a crucial component of budgeting. A financial cushion allows you to handle unexpected expenses without borrowing, contributing to financial stability.

With a budget, you can make informed spending decisions and prioritize expenses based on your financial forecasts. This clarity reduces impulsive spending and encourages thoughtful financial choices.

How to Create a Budget

1. Determine your total monthly income. Include all sources of income, such as salary, bonuses, side jobs, or investment income. This gives you a starting point for budgeting.
2. Categorize your expenses into fixed and variable categories. Fixed costs include rent or mortgage, utilities, and loan payments. Variable expenses encompass groceries, entertainment, and discretionary spending.
3. Prioritize your expenses based on importance. Essential expenses like housing, utilities, and groceries should come first. Non-essential or discretionary spending can be adjusted based on your financial goals.

Regularly track your spending and compare it to your budget. This helps identify areas where you may be overspending or where adjustments can be made. There are various budgeting tools and apps that can simplify this process.

Be flexible with your budget. Life circumstances and priorities may change, requiring adjustments to your spending plan. Regularly review and update your budget to align with your financial ambitions.

Here's an example of Laura's monthly budget:

Income: $3,000
Expenses:
- Rent: $2,000
- Utilities: $300
- Groceries: $300
- Student loan: $200
- Entertainment: $100
Remaining: $100

In this example, $100 remains at the end of each month. Also, Laura spends $100 on entertainment, like going out with friends or watching movies at the theater, which is a discretionary expense. Laura can see the relationship between her income and expenses and can make decisions to optimize her finances. For example, she might reduce her entertainment expenses to pay off her student loan much faster or create an emergency fund.

Creating a budget allows for additional benefits because you'll better understand your inflows and outflows. Here are two more advantages:

You can identify short-term and long-term financial targets. Whether paying off debt, saving for a vacation, or investing for retirement, having clear goals directs your budget.

You can establish an emergency fund to cover unexpected expenses. Aim for three to six months' living expenses to provide a financial safety net.

Budgeting Methods

Various methods can be employed to create a budget, and the choice often depends on personal preferences and financial aspirations. Here are several common budgeting approaches.

Traditional Budgeting: Allocate specific amounts to different expense categories based on your income and spending priorities.

50/30/20 Budgeting: Allocate 50% of your income to needs, 30% to wants, and 20% to savings and debt repayment.

Zero-Based Budgeting: Allocate every dollar of your income to specific categories, ensuring that your income minus expenses equals zero.

Envelope System: Allocate cash into envelopes (or jars) for specific spending categories. Once the envelope is empty, spending in that category is exhausted until the next budgeting period.

Percentage-Based Budgeting: Allocate fixed percentages of your income to different expense categories, such as housing, transportation, and savings.

Biweekly or Monthly Budgeting: Create a budget based on your pay frequency (biweekly or monthly).

Automated Budgeting Apps: Utilize budgeting apps that automatically categorize expenses, track spending, and provide insights.

Incremental Budgeting: Gradually adjust your budget based on changes in income, expenses, or financial goals—for example, a salesperson whose income fluctuates monthly.

Emergency Fund Budgeting: Prioritize building and maintaining an emergency fund before allocating funds to other spending categories.

Pay Yourself First: Allocate a portion of your income to savings and debt repayment before budgeting for other expenses.

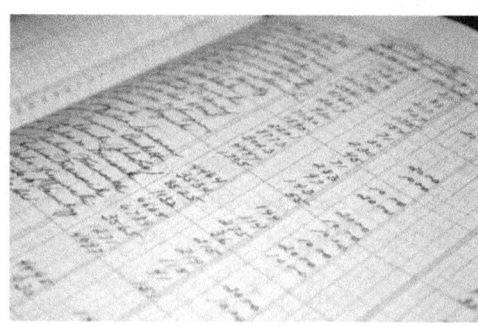

Sticking to Your Budget

The quickest way to make no progress is to create a budget and not stick to it. I get it; changing financial and spending habits can take time. However, the time is now for you to embrace a better financial future and more stability.

Set clear financial goals that your budget aims to achieve whether saving for a vacation, paying off debt, or building an emergency fund, having clear objectives provides motivation.

Ensure your budget reflects your actual income and expenses realistically. Overestimating or underestimating can lead to frustration and deviation from your financial plan.

Acknowledge and celebrate milestones along the way. Recognizing your achievements, even the small ones, reinforces positive financial behavior.

Share your budget and financial dreams with a family member, friend, or accountability partner. Discussing your progress with someone can provide support and motivation.

Goal Setting

Goal setting is fundamental to personal finance, providing a roadmap for financial success and guiding decision-making. When setting financial goals, it's essential to be specific, measurable, achievable, relevant, and time-bound (SMART is the acronym). Clear and well-defined ambitions help individuals stay focused, motivated, and in control of their financial well-being. Goals are what take us from one place to another. So, without them, we are susceptible to financial uncertainty.

Financial objectives are highly individual, and it's crucial to tailor them to your specific circumstances, priorities, and aspirations. Furthermore, your goal or goals should be achievable and driven by your budget to avoid stress.

Benefits of Goal Setting

Financial goals provide clarity about what you want to achieve with your money. They give you a clear direction and focus, helping you make intentional spending, saving, and investing decisions.

Goals serve as powerful motivators. A specific financial objective creates a sense of purpose, driving you to stay disciplined in your financial habits. This motivation can help you overcome challenges and sacrifice to achieve your desires.

Setting financial amounts helps you prioritize your spending. When you have clear objectives, you can distinguish between essential and non-essential expenses, making it easier to allocate resources efficiently.

Goals serve as the foundation for effective budgeting and financial planning. They provide a framework for creating a budget that aligns with your objectives, ensuring you allocate resources to meet your financial priorities.

Financial ambitions often include building an emergency fund. This fund is a financial safety net, providing a cushion to cover unexpected expenses without derailing your overall financial plan.

Goals related to debt repayment contribute to financial freedom and independence. By setting targets for reducing or eliminating debt, you work towards freeing up resources that can be redirected towards saving, investing, or other financial desires.

Financial goals encourage regular saving and investing. Whether saving for short-term objectives like a vacation or long-term goals like retirement, having specific objectives prompts consistent contributions to savings and investment accounts.

Goals provide a basis for measuring progress. Regularly assessing how far you've achieved your goals helps you stay on track, celebrate milestones, and adjust as needed.

With clear financial intentions, decision-making becomes more straightforward. When faced with financial choices, you can evaluate whether they align with your goals, helping you make informed and strategic decisions.

Achieving financial ambitions contributes to increased financial security. Whether it's building an emergency fund, paying off debt, or saving for retirement, each goal attained enhances your overall financial resilience.

Financial goals are essential components of a long-term financial plan. By setting and achieving these goals, you work towards long-term financial success, including financial independence and the ability to meet your future needs and aspirations.

Accomplishing financial objectives brings a sense of personal satisfaction and well-being. Knowing that you have successfully managed your money and achieved what you set out to accomplish enhances happiness and peace of mind.

Here are several examples of goals using the SMART formula.

Goal: Expense Reduction
Specific: Cut monthly discretionary spending by 20%.
Measurable: Track and analyze discretionary expenses regularly.
Achievable: Identify areas for cost reduction and adjust spending habits.
Relevant: Frees up additional funds for savings and goals.
Time-Bound: Achieve a 20% reduction in discretionary spending within three months.

Goal: Income Increase
Specific: Increase side hustle income by 25%.
Measurable: Track income from a side hustle and set specific targets.
Achievable: Explore opportunities to expand the side hustle or acquire new skills.
Relevant: Enhances overall income and financial stability.
Time-Bound: Achieve a 25% increase in my side job income within the following year.

Goal: Debt Repayment
Specific: Pay off $5,000 in high-interest credit card debt.
Measurable: Track monthly debt payments and monitor decreasing balances.
Achievable: Create a debt repayment plan and allocate additional funds from the budget.
Relevant: Reduces financial stress and saves on interest.
Time-Bound: Eliminate $5,000 in credit card debt within 18 months.

Goal: Emergency Fund
Specific: Save three months' living expenses in an emergency fund.
Measurable: Track progress monthly by setting aside a fixed amount.
Achievable: Adjust my budget to allocate a percentage of income to the emergency fund.
Relevant: Provides a financial safety net for unexpected expenses.
Time-Bound: Achieve the goal within the next 12 months.

Goal: Retirement Savings
Specific: Contribute 15% of annual income to a retirement account.
Measurable: Track annual contributions and monitor retirement account growth.
Achievable: Adjust my budget to accommodate increased retirement savings.
Relevant: Builds a robust retirement fund for future financial security.
Time-Bound: Contribute 15% annually to retirement for the next five years.

Implementation

Prioritize goals based on their importance and urgency. This helps individuals allocate resources effectively and focus on the most critical objectives.

Regularly review your progress toward each financial goal. Use financial statements, account balances, or tracking tools to monitor how close you are to achieving specific objectives. Life circumstances change, and plans may need adjustments. Be open to modifying your goals based on changes in income, family structure, or unexpected events.

Celebrate achievements along the way. Recognizing milestones, even small ones, reinforces the commitment to financial goals.

Periodically reassess your financial priorities. As circumstances evolve, your desires and priorities may shift, requiring adjustments to your financial plan.

Consider consulting with financial professionals when reviewing and adjusting goals. Financial advisors can provide insights and guidance to ensure your plan aligns with your aspirations.

Exercise: Your Budget

For this exercise, you'll create a budget. I recommend keeping your budget simple using a notepad or electronic spreadsheet like Microsoft Excel or Google Sheets. If you're up for the challenge, you may want to search for and use a budgeting app. However, sometimes, apps can derail people before they start.

Next, set two goals that you want to achieve within 12 months. Use your budget to formulate realistic goals that will impact your finances, reducing the need to live paycheck to paycheck. For example, you want to cut your expenses by 15% monthly. Also, list the activities you'll implement to achieve your goal. For instance, you'll substitute brand-name food products for generics or private labels. You'll eliminate some non-essential expenses until you can easily afford them.

Here's an expansive list of common expenses to assist your budget creation:

Housing:
Mortgage or rent
Property taxes (if not included in the mortgage)
Homeowners or renters' insurance
Home maintenance and repairs

Utilities:
Electricity
Gas
Water and sewer
Trash collection
Internet and cable/satellite TV

Groceries:
Food for home consumption
Toiletries and household supplies

Communication:
Mobile phone bills
Landline phone bills

Transportation:
Car loan or lease payments
Gasoline or public transportation costs
Auto insurance
Maintenance and repairs
Parking fees

Insurance:
Health insurance premiums
Life insurance premiums
Disability insurance premiums
Other insurance policies (e.g., dental and vision care)

Debt Payments:
Credit card payments
Student loan payments
Personal loan payments
Other loan repayments

Childcare/Dependent Care:
Daycare or childcare expenses
Babysitting or nanny costs

Health and Wellness:
Gym or fitness memberships
Prescription medications
Health-related expenses (e.g., vitamins and supplements)

Personal Care:
Haircuts and salon services
Personal grooming products

Subscription Services:
Streaming services (Netflix, Hulu, etc.)
Magazines or newspaper subscriptions
Software subscriptions

Education:
Tuition or student loan payments
Educational materials or courses

Entertainment:
Dining out and ordering in
Movies, concerts, or events
Hobbies and recreational activities

Savings:
Contributions to emergency fund
Retirement savings contributions
Other savings goals (e.g., travel or home purchase fund)

Miscellaneous:
Clothing and personal items
Gifts or charitable donations
Pet expenses (food, veterinary care, etc.)

Taxes:
Income taxes (if not withheld from your paycheck)
Property taxes (if not included in the mortgage)

Financial Fees:
Bank fees
Credit card fees
Investment account fees

Chapter 4
MINDING YOUR MEANS

You're living beyond your means if you earn $45,000 annually and spend $45,001. Similarly, the same is true if you earn $6,000 monthly and spend $6,001.

Living beyond your means refers to individuals or households that spend more money than their incomes can comfortably support. This often leads to expenses exceeding the available resources, resulting in a reliance on credit or accumulating debt to maintain a particular lifestyle.

This chapter reviews common causes and solutions for excessive spending to align your income and expenses.

Causes and Solutions

No Budget

A budget acts as a compass to guide your inflows and outflows. So, without a budget, individuals may not clearly understand their income, expenses, and overall financial situation. This lack of awareness can make making informed and responsible financial decisions challenging.

A budget allows individuals to prioritize their spending based on essential needs and financial goals. Without this structure, allocating funds impulsively, neglecting critical financial obligations, and spending on non-essential items is risky.

Budgets provide a tool for effective financial planning. Without a plan, individuals may struggle to navigate unexpected financial challenges or plan for future expenses, leading to a higher risk of living beyond their means.

Solution: Creating and maintaining a budget is essential to avoid living beyond one's means. A budget encourages responsible spending and empowers individuals to make informed financial decisions, ultimately contributing to a more stable and secure financial future.

Lack of Discipline

Financial discipline involves making decisions that align with long-term goals and priorities, even when faced with short-term temptations or difficulties. Without it, individuals may be caught in a cycle of overspending and financial chaos.

Without discipline, it's easy to give in to impulse purchases, buying items on a whim rather than based on need or planned decision-making. This can lead to spending money that should be allocated to essential expenses or savings.

The temptation to use credit cards for immediate gratification rather than as a tool for planned purchases can lead to accumulating debt. Individuals may incur high interest and fees without discipline to pay off balances in full, exacerbating their financial strain.

Creating and sticking to a budget requires discipline. Without it, there's a tendency to overspend in various categories without tracking or controlling expenses, making living within one's means difficult.

Financial discipline is crucial in setting and achieving short-term and long-term financial goals. Lack of discipline makes it challenging to progress towards significant objectives like buying a home, investing, or saving for retirement.

A lack of discipline can justify unnecessary expenses as needs rather than wants. This rationalization can lead to prioritizing discretionary spending over essential financial commitments and desires.

Discipline is necessary to address financial issues proactively. Without it, there may be a tendency to ignore or postpone dealing with financial problems, allowing them to worsen over time.

Without the discipline to control spending, any increase in income can lead to proportional increases in spending, a phenomenon known as lifestyle inflation. This prevents improving one's financial situation, even with higher earnings.

Solution: Cultivating financial discipline involves creating a budget, setting clear financial targets, distinguishing between wants and needs, and developing habits that support long-term economic health, such as saving regularly and managing debt wisely. Building financial discipline is a gradual process, but it's essential for avoiding the pitfalls of living beyond one's means and achieving financial stability and freedom.

Consumerism

Consumerism, characterized by a culture that places a high value on acquiring goods and services, can contribute significantly to living beyond your means. This phenomenon is driven by the constant pursuit of material possessions, often fueled by marketing, social pressure, and a desire for instant gratification.

Consumerism promotes the idea that acquiring more possessions leads to happiness or social status. This can result in impulsive spending on non-essential items, often driven by the desire for the latest trends or lifestyle upgrades.

The social aspect of consumerism often involves comparing oneself to others and striving to maintain a particular lifestyle. This can lead to overspending to keep up with friends, neighbors, or societal expectations, even when it exceeds one's financial capacity. This is often referred to as "keeping up with the Joneses."

Consumerism tends to emphasize the fulfillment of wants rather than needs. Individuals influenced by this mindset may prioritize discretionary spending on luxury items, entertainment, or non-essential services over essential expenses and financial responsibilities.

Consumerism often provides a fleeting sense of satisfaction derived from acquiring new possessions. This can lead to a continuous cycle of seeking temporary happiness through purchases without considering the long-term financial impact.

A strong focus on material possessions and pursuing a lavish lifestyle can lead individuals to prioritize spending on tangible items over building financial security, saving, or investing for the future.

Aggressive advertising and marketing campaigns play a significant role in promoting consumerism. The constant exposure to messages that highlight the desirability of products can contribute to impulsive buying and reckless spending.

In some societies, consumerism is deeply ingrained in cultural expectations. Keeping up with societal norms and expectations can pressure individuals to spend beyond their means to meet perceived standards of success and happiness.

Consumerism often leads to overconsumption, contributing to environmental issues such as waste and resource depletion. Ironically, excessive consumerism can have broader consequences beyond personal finance.

Solution: To mitigate the adverse effects of consumerism on personal finances, individuals can adopt a more mindful and intentional approach to spending. This includes distinguishing between wants and needs, creating a budget, practicing delayed gratification, and prioritizing financial goals over short-term material desires. Building financial literacy and resilience can empower individuals to resist the pressures of consumerism and make informed decisions that align with their long-term financial wellness.

Another growing trend is minimalism, focusing on embracing quality over quantity. Minimalists carefully select items, ensuring everything owned serves a purpose and enhances their experience. Additionally, a minimalist lifestyle identifies what is essential in your life and has the courage to eliminate the rest.

Social and Peer Pressure

Social and peer pressure can significantly influence an individual's financial decisions, often leading to the temptation of living beyond one's means. The desire to conform to societal expectations or meet the standards set by peers can create financial habits that may not align with one's actual financial capacity.

Individuals often compare their lifestyles to those of their peers or social circles. The pressure to maintain or elevate one's standard of living to match others can lead to increased spending on non-essential items, status goods, or experiences that may not be affordable.

The fear of missing out on social events, gatherings, or experiences can drive impulsive spending. Individuals may feel compelled to participate in activities or purchase items to avoid feeling left out, even if it strains their budget.

Social and peer pressure often encourages individuals to stay current with trends and fads. This can result in regular purchases of fashionable items, even if short-lived, leading to a continuous cycle of spending.

Milestones and achievements among peers, such as weddings, vacations, or extravagant celebrations, can create pressure to match or exceed these experiences. Individuals may overspend on similar events to maintain a sense of social parity.

Seeking approval from peers can influence spending decisions. Individuals may be inclined to buy products or services endorsed by their social circles, regardless of whether these align with their needs, ideals, or financial priorities.

The desire for social status or acceptance can drive spending on status symbols, such as designer clothing, luxury accessories, or high-end gadgets. This pursuit of status may lead to financial strain as individuals prioritize external validation over financial pragmatism.

Social circles often create a perception of each individual's wealth or financial success. Individuals may feel compelled to project a specific image, leading to spending beyond their means to maintain or enhance their perceived financial standing.

Envy or jealousy resulting from perceived financial success among peers can trigger a desire to emulate that success. This may lead individuals to spend in ways that mimic the lifestyles of others without considering the potential financial consequences.

Social media platforms can amplify social and peer pressure by showcasing curated images of seemingly perfect lifestyles. Constant exposure to these images may create unrealistic expectations, prompting individuals to overspend to emulate the portrayed lifestyles.

Solution: To counter the impact of social and peer pressure, individuals can prioritize financial literacy, establish personal financial goals, and communicate openly about their financial boundaries with friends and peers. Developing a strong sense of financial independence and focusing on long-term financial health can help individuals resist the pressures that may lead to living beyond their means.

Problem Avoidance

Problem avoidance can contribute to living beyond one's means, as individuals may resort to unhealthy coping mechanisms, such as excessive spending, to escape or distract themselves from underlying issues.

Facing challenging situations, like a bad relationship or personal issues, may evoke negative emotions. Some individuals shop to alleviate stress, sadness, or frustration temporarily. This emotional spending can lead to impulsive purchases and increased financial strain.

Shopping can be perceived as a form of "retail therapy," where individuals seek comfort or distraction from problems by indulging in the excitement of purchasing new items. This behavior may provide short-term emotional relief but often results in financial consequences.

Avoiding problems by engaging in excessive consumption creates a cycle of using material possessions to escape reality. This can lead to habitual spending patterns, contributing to debt accumulation and hindering financial stability.

Problem avoidance may manifest as compulsive buying behaviors, where individuals continuously acquire items without genuine need. This compulsiveness can lead to a cycle of overspending and hoarding, as buying becomes a temporary distraction from underlying issues.

Individuals practicing problem avoidance may deny or downplay their financial challenges, creating a disconnect between their spending habits and the actual state of their finances. This denial can lead to continued overspending without addressing the root causes.

While shopping may temporarily distract or relieve underlying problems, it doesn't address the root causes. As a result, the initial issues persist, and individuals find themselves in a continuous cycle of spending without resolving the underlying problems.

Solution: To break the cycle of problem avoidance and its financial consequences, individuals can consider healthier coping strategies, such as seeking professional help, engaging in open communication with loved ones, and addressing the root causes of stress or dissatisfaction. Developing emotional resilience and financial awareness can empower individuals to make conscious, positive choices, contributing to their emotional, mental, and economic stability.

Needs Versus Wants

Understanding the differences between needs and wants is vital in your financial arsenal. With this knowledge, individuals can establish a clear financial hierarchy, make informed spending decisions, and work toward achieving financial goals while maintaining economic stability.

Needs are essential for survival and well-being. They are the necessities required to maintain a reasonable standard of living. These include:

- Basic Shelter: A safe and secure place to live.
- Food: Nutritious sustenance necessary for health.
- Clothing: Appropriate attire for protection and comfort.
- Healthcare: Essential medical care and health-related expenses.
- Education: Basic education required for personal development.

Conversely, wants are desires that enhance our quality of life but are not necessary for survival. They represent our preferences, aspirations, and lifestyle choices. Examples of wants include:

- Luxury Items: High-end goods and services that go beyond necessities.
- Entertainment: Non-essential leisure activities such as dining out, travel, and entertainment subscriptions.

- Fashion and Accessories: Items beyond basic clothing needs, like designer labels or luxury accessories.
- Technology Upgrades: The latest gadgets or devices that may not be essential for daily functioning.
- Hobbies and Recreation: Pursuits that contribute to personal enjoyment but are not necessary for well-being.

Here are some examples of how categorizing needs and wants can help you.

Budgeting
Needs: Prioritizing needs in your budget ensures that essential expenses are covered first, providing a foundation for financial strength.
Wants: Allocating discretionary income for wants allows for enjoyment without jeopardizing financial security.

Spending
Needs: Addressing needs first prevents neglect of essential areas and contributes to overall welfare.
Wants: Prioritizing wants based on available discretionary income avoids overspending and supports responsible financial habits.

Reduce Unnecessary Costs or Wants

Cutting unnecessary costs will help you balance your books. Here are strategies to help you identify and reduce unnecessary expenses.

- Review your spending habits and identify non-essential or discretionary expenses.
- Negotiate with service providers, such as cable, internet, or insurance companies, to lower your bills. Mention competitor offers or express your loyalty to secure discounts.

- Limit eating out at restaurants and opt for homemade meals. Plan your meals and consider batch cooking to save both time and money.
- Consider cutting traditional cable or satellite TV services and explore more affordable streaming options. Choose services that align with your viewing preferences.
- Evaluate magazine subscriptions, memberships, or clubs that may no longer provide significant value. Cancel or downgrade memberships that you do not fully utilize. Consider cheaper alternatives for services you want to keep.
- Implement energy-saving practices to reduce utility bills. Use energy-efficient appliances and consider upgrading insulation in your home.
- Explore public transportation, carpooling, or biking to reduce fuel and maintenance costs. Consider downsizing to a more fuel-efficient vehicle.
- Learn basic home maintenance tasks to avoid hiring professionals for minor repairs. DIY projects can save money and enhance your skills.

Exercise: Live Within Your Means

If you live beyond your means, one or multiple reasons discussed in this chapter might relate to you. If so, take note and list up to five activities you'll take to address it. Your actions can be short or long-term to bring your monthly finances into balance. Secondly, identify up to five "wants" they you purchase frequently, for example, a Starbucks coffee. Temporarily suspend these purchases until your financial situation improves.

Chapter 5
High Costs: Manhattan

The cost of living in some cities is too hard to fathom. New York (Manhattan) is a prime example of that. According to one survey, the New York borough's cost of living is 24% more than Honolulu's, the second-most expensive urban area in the U.S., and 31% higher than San Francisco's, the third-most expensive city. Therefore, Manhattan residents with low incomes will struggle.

Living beyond or within your means is in your control compared to living in a city or state with a high cost of living. Still, there are options to combat high living costs, which we'll cover in this chapter.

Cost of Living Factors

Several factors contribute to a city's high cost of living, making it more expensive for residents to cover their basic needs and maintain a certain standard of living. These factors can vary from one location to another, but some common contributors include:

Housing: High demand and limited housing supply can drive up real estate prices, making renting or purchasing a home expensive. Housing shortages exist in multiple North American cities, including San Francisco and Toronto. Places with higher property taxes and maintenance costs contribute to the overall cost of housing.

Utilities: Electricity, gas, and water prices can significantly impact living expenses.

Cities with expensive waste disposal services may pass those costs on to residents.

Transportation: Cities with high fuel prices contribute to elevated transportation costs. The availability and cost of public transit can influence the overall transportation expenses for residents.

Healthcare: Areas with higher healthcare costs, including insurance premiums and out-of-pocket expenses, contribute to the cost of living. The availability and quality of medical facilities can impact healthcare costs.

Education: Cities with prestigious or well-funded educational institutions may have higher tuition and fees. For towns with universities, the cost of living may be affected by the accommodations and services available to students.

Food Prices: The price of groceries, influenced by transportation, agricultural practices, and local taxes, can contribute to higher living costs.

Taxes: Income tax rates at the local level can impact disposable income. Cities with higher sales tax rates increase the cost of goods and services.

Entertainment and Recreation: Cities with a vibrant cultural scene and numerous events may cost more. The availability and quality of recreational facilities can contribute to overall costs.

Quality of Life Amenities: Cities with well-maintained parks and green spaces may have higher costs associated with their upkeep. Cities investing in safety measures may have higher related costs.

Cost of Doing Business: Higher business costs, including rent for commercial spaces, may be passed on to consumers. Cities with higher business taxes may see an impact on the price of goods and services.

Given these factors, it's no wonder Manhattan is expensive. It's a cosmopolitan city with a rich history, exciting vibe, impressive architecture, a global financial hub, daily cultural and social events, business opportunities, and more. Also, it's one of the leading international travel destinations.

Even if you don't live in Manhattan, you might live somewhere costlier than the national average. Therefore, your living costs might contribute to living beyond your means. Either way, let's review some actions you can take to decrease your living costs.

Reducing Costs

Reduce Everyday Expenses

Review your budget for everyday expenses you can reduce to lower your living costs. However, unless the expenses are significant, their impact may be insufficient.

Relocate

Relocating or moving to a different place can be a strategy to combat high living costs. Still, it involves carefully considering various factors, including job prospects, lifestyle preferences, and potential trade-offs.

Different places have different costs for housing, groceries, and transportation. People can often save money by moving to a more affordable city, town, or region. Moving to an area with less expensive homes or apartments can significantly reduce living costs. Achieving financial goals, such as saving for a home or retirement, may be more attainable in a location with a lower cost of living.

With the rise of remote work, people may live in areas with lower living costs while maintaining employment with companies in more expensive regions.

Downsize

Downsizing refers to reducing the size or scale of something. In the context of living arrangements, it typically means moving to a smaller and more cost-effective home or lifestyle.

Moving to a smaller home often comes with lower associated costs, including mortgage or rent, property taxes, utilities, and maintenance. This can result in significant savings over time.

Downsizing may involve decluttering and simplifying one's lifestyle by eliminating unnecessary possessions. This reduces physical clutter and can lead to financial decluttering by cutting expenses associated with maintaining a larger living space.

Smaller homes typically require less energy to heat or cool. This can lead to reduced utility bills, contributing to overall cost savings.

A smaller home often means fewer maintenance responsibilities. This can result in lower costs for repairs and upkeep, freeing up funds for other financial priorities.

If homeowners downsize by selling a larger property, they may be able to unlock home equity. This money can be used to pay off debts, invest, or fund other financial plans.

Downsizing may be prompted by changes in family size, such as children moving out, or changes in personal circumstances, such as retirement. Adapting living arrangements to suit current needs better can lead to financial advantages.

Smaller living spaces often mean simplified financial management. With fewer bills and responsibilities, individuals may find it easier to stay organized and on top of their finances.

Some people choose to downsize by transitioning from homeownership to renting. Renting can offer flexibility and may come with fewer financial responsibilities than owning a property. However, renting removes your ability to control costs since rental prices are at the discretion of property owners.

Boost Income

Increasing your income won't lower your costs per se, but earning a higher income will reduce the percentage allocated to monthly expenses, making it a viable strategy.

Share Expenses

Do you have a spare room to rent? While inviting a tenant into your home is a valid option to share and reduce living expenses, I kept it to the end because it warrants serious consideration.

Living with strangers or roommates isn't for everyone and terrible tenants can worsen matters. Search "rental horror stories" to understand what I mean. Still, qualified and trustworthy tenants will bring money and company into your life.

If you do want to consider this option, it's critical to research tenants' rights and how to set yourself up for success. The last thing you want to do is chase your roomie for rent money.

Here are the pros and cons of renting to reduce expenses.

Pros:

Renting a room is often more cost-effective than renting an entire apartment or house. This can significantly reduce living expenses and allow individuals to allocate their budget to other financial priorities.

Utilities and other shared expenses can be divided among the roommates, leading to lower individual costs. This sharing of financial responsibilities can contribute to overall savings.

Renting a room provides flexibility, especially for those needing short-term living arrangements. It allows individuals to adapt to changing circumstances without a long-term lease commitment.

Roommates often share household chores and responsibilities, saving time and effort for everyone involved.

Living with roommates can provide social opportunities and companionship. It can be particularly beneficial for those new to an area or looking to build a social network.

A shared living arrangement may provide access to amenities like a fully furnished living space, appliances, and other shared facilities.

Cons:

One of the main drawbacks is the potential lack of privacy. Sharing living space with others means compromising personal space and less controlling the environment.

Differences in lifestyle, habits, and preferences among roommates can lead to conflicts. Compatibility is crucial, and incompatible living situations can be stressful and challenging.

Financial arrangements, such as rent payments and shared expenses, depend on the cooperation of roommates. If one roommate fails to contribute, it can strain the living situation for everyone.

Roommates may have different preferences for temperature, noise levels, or cleanliness. This lack of control over the living environment can be a source of frustration.

Lease agreements may be in the name of one primary tenant, making it challenging for others to enforce their rights or have a say in decisions related to the property.

Shared living arrangements can be more transient, with roommates coming and going. This may lead to a less stable living environment, especially for those seeking long-term stability.

While shared responsibilities can be a pro, they can also be a con if there's a lack of cooperation among roommates. Unequal distribution of chores or financial obligations can lead to tension.

Renting a room may involve legal considerations, especially if the primary tenant is responsible for the lease. Understanding the legal implications is crucial to avoid potential conflicts.

Tips for Finding an Excellent Roommate

Finding an excellent tenant or roommate is crucial for maintaining a positive and stable living environment. Whether you're a landlord looking to rent out a property or an individual searching for a roommate, here are some tips to help you find a reliable and compatible tenant:

Provide a clear and detailed listing for your property, including information about rent, lease terms, amenities, and any specific requirements. Transparency from the beginning helps attract suitable candidates.

Implement a thorough screening process. Conduct background checks, verify employment and income, and check references from previous landlords. This helps ensure that you are selecting a responsible tenant.

Communicate your expectations regarding rent payments, maintenance responsibilities, and house rules. This helps set the groundwork for a positive landlord-tenant relationship.

Require potential tenants to fill out a comprehensive rental application. This document should include their rental history, employment, and references.

Conduct face-to-face interviews with potential tenants. This lets you gauge their personality, communication skills, and whether they would fit the property well.

Contact previous landlords to inquire about the applicant's rental history. This can provide insights into their reliability as a tenant.

Create a well-defined lease agreement that outlines all terms and conditions, including rent amount, due dates, and any rules or expectations. Ensure that both parties thoroughly understand and agree to the terms.

Collect a security deposit before the tenant moves in. This provides a financial safety net for any potential damage to the property.

If a potential tenant or roommate doesn't have a rental history or references or seems unwilling to pay a deposit, these are signs of possible problems. It would be best if you avoided these people at all costs.

Exercise: Reduce Living Costs

Are high costs of living impacting your finances or stressing you out? If yes, which option in this chapter can improve your situation the most? What are your preferred option's pros, cons, and time horizon?

Research and create a plan that aligns with your financial goals.

Chapter 6
THE DEBT TERMINATOR

Another day, another credit card statement, and it seems you're not progressing on your outstanding debt. That is the reality of millions who spend first and think later while using credit to fund purchases.

Debt can be a blessing or a curse, depending on how you manage it. As a blessing, credit serves as a financial lifeline when you need it or a way to rack up rewards or cashback. Many individuals in this group pay off their credit in full immediately, limiting additional costs like interest. When credit is used irresponsibly, in desperation, or without financial knowledge, it can become a curse, leading to further debt, financial hell, and low credit scores.

Let's review consumer debt—using credit cards, credit lines, and personal loans—since it's a common cause of financial struggles. Later, we'll review mortgage debt.

Debt Fundamentals

Debt occurs when you borrow money from another party under the agreement that you will pay it back later, usually with interest. Interest is the cost of borrowing money and is typically expressed as a percentage. For instance, Jack borrows $500 at a 21% interest rate using his credit card. If he pays back the debt in full on or before June 3rd, he won't get charged interest. If he pays back less than the total amount, interest will be calculated on the amount outstanding.

The interest rate is a critical component of any debt. It can significantly affect the total amount you will end up paying back. Interest rates can be fixed, remaining constant over the life of the loan, or variable, changing at specific intervals.

Types of Debt

There are several types of debt, each with its characteristics and uses:

- Secured debt is backed by collateral, meaning the borrower pledges an asset (like a house or car) as security for the loan. If the borrower fails to repay, the lender can seize the asset. Mortgages and auto loans are common examples.
- Unsecured debt doesn't require collateral. Lenders offer this loan based on your creditworthiness and promise to repay. Credit cards and student loans are typical examples.
- Revolving debt allows you to borrow up to a specific limit and repay it, then borrow again. Credit cards are the most common form of revolving debt.
- Installment Debt: This involves borrowing and repaying a fixed amount in scheduled payments over a set period. Mortgages, auto loans, and personal loans fall into this category.

Credit Score

A credit score is a numerical representation of an individual's creditworthiness. It's based on various factors in their credit history and financial behavior. The most common credit scoring model is the FICO score, which ranges from 300 to 850. Factors influencing credit score include:

- Payment History (a 35% weighting): Timely payments on credit accounts contribute positively.
- Credit Utilization (30%): The ratio of current credit card balances to credit limits.
- Length of Credit History (15%): The average age of credit accounts.

- Types of Credit in Use (10%): The mix of credit accounts (credit cards, mortgages, etc.).
- New Credit (10%): Recent credit inquiries and newly opened accounts.

A higher credit score indicates lower credit risk. Borrowers with higher scores are perceived as more likely to repay debts, making them eligible for lower interest rates. By contrast, a lower credit score suggests higher credit risk. Borrowers with lower scores may be charged higher interest rates to compensate for the perceived risk.

Credit History

Credit history is a detailed record of an individual's borrowing and repayment activities. It includes information about credit accounts, payment history, outstanding balances, and derogatory marks such as late payments or bankruptcies. Factors affecting credit history include:

- Credit Accounts: The types and number of credit accounts a person has.
- Payment History: Records of on-time or late payments.

- Credit Inquiries: Instances when someone checks the credit report.
- Derogatory Marks: Negative items like bankruptcies or collections.

A favorable credit history, consistent on-time payments, and responsible credit management contribute to a higher credit score, resulting in lower interest rates. Conversely, adverse items in a credit history, such as late payments or defaults, can lower the credit score, leading to higher interest rates or difficulty in obtaining credit.

Interest Rates

Lenders use credit scores and history to assess the risk of lending money. The interest rate offered reflects this perceived risk.

A higher credit score and positive credit history signal financial responsibility and trustworthiness to lenders, increasing the likelihood of receiving favorable interest rates.

Regularly monitoring your credit report allows you to identify inaccuracies, address issues promptly, and maintain or improve your creditworthiness over time.

Boost Your Credit Score for Lower Interest Rates

Boosting your credit score gradually requires responsible financial habits and strategic actions. Start by consistently paying bills on time, as your payment history is a significant factor in your credit score.

Aim to reduce credit card balances to below 30% of the credit limit, as a lower credit utilization ratio positively influences your score.

Be cautious about opening too many new accounts, which can negatively impact your average account age.

If necessary, check your credit report for errors or fraud and dispute inaccuracies.

Maintain a diverse mix of credit types, such as credit cards and installment loans, to positively impact your score.

Negotiate lower interest rates with creditors, especially if you have a good payment history.

Consider becoming an authorized user on someone else's well-managed credit account to benefit from their positive credit history.

Resolve outstanding collections and settle debts to reduce negative items on your credit report.

Responsible use of secured credit cards can help build a positive credit history, and keeping older credit accounts open, even with a zero balance, lengthens credit history.

Compounding Interest

Compounding interest involves earning or paying interest not only on the initial principal amount but also on the accumulated interest from previous periods. In simple terms, it's interest on interest, and it can work to amplify the growth of savings or the cost of debt over time.

For individuals with high-interest debt, like credit cards or certain types of loans, compound interest can lead to a rapidly growing debt balance. If only minimum payments are made, the interest continues to compound, making it challenging to escape the debt cycle.

Compound interest magnifies over time, especially with long-term investments or loans. This means that decisions made early regarding saving or borrowing can substantially impact one's financial situation years or even decades later.

When individuals cannot make significant payments towards their debt, the compounding effect can lead to a situation where the debt grows faster than they can manage. This can result in prolonged debt repayment periods and higher overall interest costs.

Effective Debt Management

Effective debt management involves financial knowledge, discipline, and strategic planning. By paying on time, understanding the terms, prioritizing high-interest debt, and avoiding unnecessary borrowing, individuals can work towards reducing debt and achieving greater financial independence. Let's review these factors in more detail.

Pay on Time

Importance: Timely payments are crucial for maintaining a positive credit history and avoiding penalties. Late payments can lead to late fees and increased interest rates, negatively impacting your credit score.

Impact on Credit Score: Payment history is a significant factor in credit scoring models. Consistently making on-time payments demonstrates financial responsibility and positively contributes to your credit score.

Action Steps:
• Set up automatic payments or reminders to ensure payments are made on or before the due date.
• Contact creditors immediately if you anticipate difficulty paying to discuss potential solutions.

Understand the Terms

Importance: Knowing the terms of any debt you take on is crucial for making informed financial decisions. It helps you understand the cost of borrowing, potential fees, and the overall financial commitment.

Interest Rates: Understand whether the interest rate is fixed or variable.

Repayment Terms: Be aware of the duration of the loan and any associated fees for early repayment or late payments.

Action Steps:

- Carefully review loan agreements, credit card terms, or any financial contracts before agreeing to the terms.
- Ask questions to clarify terms, details, or conditions that may not be clear.

Prioritize High-Interest Debt

Importance: High-interest debt, such as credit card balances with high APRs, can accumulate significant interest over time. Prioritizing repayment of these debts helps save money on interest payments.

Impact on Finances: Focusing on high-interest debt first allows you to free up more money in your budget for other financial goals once these high-cost debts are paid off.

Action Steps:
- List your debts, noting the interest rates associated with each.
- Allocate extra funds to pay off the highest interest rate debt first while maintaining minimum payments on others.

Avoid Unnecessary Debt

Importance: Only borrowing what you need and can confidently repay is crucial for preventing financial strain. Avoiding unnecessary debt helps you maintain better control over your finances and reduces the risk of overextending yourself.

Assessing Needs vs. Wants: Before taking on any debt, determine whether it is for a necessity or a discretionary purchase. Borrowing for essential needs may be justified, but discretionary spending should be carefully evaluated.

Action Steps:
- Create a budget to understand your financial needs and obligations.
- Differentiate between essential expenses and discretionary spending to make informed borrowing decisions.

Debt Elimination Strategies

Each of the strategies we're about to review has advantages and can be suitable depending on your circumstances, including the amount of debt, types of debt, income level, and personal financial goals.

You can research or speak with a financial representative about how these methods impact your credit score. For example, consolidating debt can lower your monthly payments but also cause a temporary dip in your credit score. The drop will come from a hard inquiry on your credit reports every time you apply for credit. The decrease usually is less than five points, and your score should rebound within a few months. Alternatively, reducing expenses or boosting your income won't impact your credit score.

Debt Snowball Method

Strategy: Pay off debts from smallest to largest, regardless of interest rate. Once the smallest debt is paid off, move to the next smallest, creating a "snowball effect."

Example: You have three debts: $500, $2,000, and $10,000. You focus on paying off the $500 debt first, then the $2,000, and finally the $10,000.

Debt Avalanche Method

Strategy: Pay off debts with the highest interest rates first, regardless of the balance. This method saves you the most money in interest over time.

Example: If you have debts with interest rates of 18%, 9%, and 4%, you will prioritize the debt with the 18% interest rate, then move to 9%, and finally to 4%.

The Snowflake Method

Strategy: Apply unexpected funds to your debt as soon as they come in rather than waiting to accumulate a significant amount.
Example: Using money from a tax refund or a bonus at work to immediately reduce your debt balance.

Debt Consolidation

Strategy: Combine multiple debts into a single debt with a lower interest rate, making payments more manageable.
Example: Taking out a personal loan at a lower interest rate to pay off multiple credit card debts.

Personal Loan

Strategy: Take out a personal loan with a lower interest rate to pay off high-interest debts.
Example: Securing a personal loan with a 7% interest rate to pay off credit card debt accruing at 20% interest.

Balance Transfer

Strategy: Transfer high-interest credit card debt to a card with a lower interest rate, often with a 0% introductory rate.
Example: Moving your credit card balance to a new card that offers a 0% annual percentage rate for 18 months.

Negotiate Lower Interest Rates

Strategy: Contact creditors to negotiate lower interest rates on your debts, reducing the interest accrued.
Example: Successfully reducing the interest rate on a credit card from 18% to 15% through negotiation with the credit card company.

Make Biweekly Payments Instead of Monthly

Strategy: Make half-payments every two weeks instead of one full payment monthly. Since there are 12 months in a year, this results in 26 half-payments, thus paying off debt faster.

Example: Splitting your monthly mortgage or loan payment in half and paying every two weeks, reducing the principal balance more quickly and saving on interest.

Cut Expenses

Strategy: Reduce monthly spending to free up more money for debt repayment.

Example: Canceling subscriptions, dining out less, and switching to cheaper utility providers to save money that can be directed toward debt payments.

Increase Income

Strategy: Seek ways to increase your income, such as taking on a part-time job, freelancing, or selling unwanted items.

Example: Using earnings from a side hustle to make extra debt payments.

Use Windfalls Wisely

Strategy: Use unexpected large sums of money, like inheritances, tax refunds, or bonuses, to pay down debt.

Example: Applying a tax refund of $3,000 directly to your highest-interest debt instead of spending it.

Mortgage Debt

A mortgage is a type of loan specifically used to finance the purchase of real estate. In a mortgage agreement, the borrower (often a homebuyer) obtains funds from a lender (typically a bank or mortgage company) to buy a property. The borrower agrees to repay the loan over a specified period, making regular payments, including principal and interest. The property itself serves as collateral for the loan. If the borrower fails to make the agreed-upon payments, the lender may have the right to take possession of the property through a legal process known as foreclosure.

Mortgages can vary in terms of interest rates, repayment periods (commonly 15 or 30 years), and other terms. The interest rate may be fixed, staying the same throughout the loan term, or variable, adjusting periodically based on market conditions. Mortgages play a crucial role in enabling individuals to achieve homeownership by spreading the cost of a property over an extended period, making homeownership more accessible to a broader population.

Mortgage Refinancing

Mortgage refinancing replaces an existing mortgage with a new one, typically to secure better terms, such as a lower interest rate or different loan duration. Homeowners may refinance for various reasons, including reducing monthly payments, consolidating debt, or tapping into home equity for other financial needs.

Benefits

- Refinancing when interest rates are lower can reduce monthly payments and overall interest costs.
- Extending the loan term may decrease monthly payments, providing short-term relief for homeowners facing financial challenges.
- Refinancing allows the consolidation of high-interest debts into a mortgage with a potentially lower interest rate.

Drawbacks

- Refinancing typically involves closing costs, which can offset the potential savings. Calculating the break-even point is essential to determine if refinancing makes financial sense.
- Stretching the loan term may lower monthly payments but could result in paying more interest over the life of the loan.
- Refinancing can affect credit scores, especially if it involves opening a new credit account or closing an existing one.

Here's an example of mortgage refinancing.

Consider a homeowner with a $300,000 mortgage at a 5% interest rate with 25 years remaining on the loan. Monthly principal and interest payments would be approximately $1,752. If the homeowner refinances at a 4% interest rate over 30 years, the new monthly payment would be around $1,432.

Calculation:
Original Loan: $300,000, 5% interest, 25 years remaining.
Monthly Payment: $1,752.

Refinanced Loan:
Refinanced Amount: $300,000.
New Interest Rate: 4%.
New Loan Term: 30 years.
New Monthly Payment: $1,432.

Savings:
Monthly Savings: $1,752 minus $1,432 = $320.
Annual Savings: $320 multiplied by 12 months = $3,840.

In this example, the homeowner lowers their monthly expenses by refinancing to a lower interest rate and extending the loan term. However, weighing the long-term costs and benefits is crucial, considering factors like closing costs, overall interest payments, and individual financial ambitions.

Mortgage refinancing warrants serious consideration to improve your payment terms and cut expenses. It can significantly improve your financial health because of the amounts involved.

Exercise: Kick Debt Butt

Debt is usually not your friend but the enemy between you and prosperity. Alternatively, debt can be an ally to improve your income, career, and life prospects, for example, paying for a course to develop new skills or renovating your home to increase its value.

Develop a debt reduction/elimination plan for this activity for the next 12 months. Include three to five strategies that apply to your circumstances and will have the most significant impact.

MELANIE NEWELL

Chapter 7
MORE MONEY, FEWER PROBLEMS

Sometimes, it can seem like your earnings are too low to cover monthly expenses and debt. Your budget will reveal if insufficient income is a problem in your finances. Should that be the case, this chapter outlines strategies to boost your income.

Increase Your Income

Who doesn't want to make more money? Most people want to because higher incomes can afford better lifestyles, health, and financial security. Also, let's face it: if you could boost your income by two or three times with the snap of a finger, much or all your expenses would become less burdensome, and living paycheck to paycheck would come to a screeching halt.

It's easier to cut expenses than it is to increase income. Still, everyday ways to make more money include the following:

- Get a salary increase (stay in your current role).
- Get a salary increase (get a promotion and advance your career).
- Switch companies or industries.
- Get a side job.
- Learn and monetize new skills.

Let's cover each of these methods in more detail.

Get a Salary Increase - Stay in Your Current Role

Securing a salary increase is a strategic process that involves preparation, timing, and negotiation. The most critical steps are understanding why you deserve a raise and convincing someone, like your manager, to give it to you.

Even if the outcome isn't what you hoped for, the process can provide valuable insights into your career development path and future opportunities at the company.

Here are steps you can take to increase your chances of successfully getting a salary increase:

Assess the Landscape

Company Performance: How is your company doing? Are sales increasing, stagnant, or declining? How is your division or department performing? Is your company hiring, taking a pause, or laying off employees? These questions are critical to assess the prospects of getting a raise and the timing of your request. You might consider switching companies or industries for a higher salary if things don't look good.

Research and Prepare

Understand Your Worth: Use salary surveys, online salary calculators, and industry benchmarks to determine the typical compensation for your role in your geographic area and industry.

Assess Your Performance: Gather concrete examples of your contributions, achievements, and any additional responsibilities you've taken on since your last salary review.

Know the Company's Pay Practices: Understand how your company handles pay increases, including the typical schedule for salary reviews and any budget constraints.

Build Your Case

Document Your Achievements: Create a detailed list of your accomplishments, quantifying them with data whenever possible (e.g., revenue generated, costs saved, projects completed).

Highlight Your Value: Focus on how your work benefits the company, including any unique skills or expertise you bring to your role.

Prepare to Address Counterarguments: Anticipate your employer's hesitations about granting a raise and prepare reasoned responses.

Choose the Right Timing

Consider Company Performance: Requesting a raise is often more effective when the company performs well financially.

Align with Performance Reviews: Timing your request around performance reviews can be strategic, as compensation adjustments are often considered during these periods.

Be Mindful of External Factors: Economic downturns, industry trends, and company-specific challenges can impact your request's success.

Practice Your Pitch

Prepare Your Talking Points: Organize your thoughts and prepare to articulate your request, the justification for the increase, and your career contributions.

Practice Out Loud: Rehearse your pitch to a trusted friend or mentor and seek feedback to refine your delivery.

Schedule a Meeting

Request a Formal Meeting: Rather than springing the conversation unexpectedly, ask your manager for a meeting to discuss your performance and compensation.

Choose an Appropriate Setting: Ensure the meeting is scheduled at a time and place where a confidential discussion can occur without interruptions.

Negotiate

Be Professional and Direct: Start the conversation by expressing your appreciation for your role and the opportunities you've been given. Then, transition into discussing your performance and request for a salary increase.

Use Your Research: Present your compiled data and achievements to justify your request.

Be Ready to Discuss Specifics: Be prepared to suggest a specific salary increase based on your research, but be open to negotiation.

Handle the Response Gracefully

If Yes: Thank your manager and ask for details on when the new salary will take effect.

If Maybe: Ask what steps you can take to work towards a raise in the future.

If No: Seek constructive feedback on improving and possibly discussing non-monetary compensation adjustments (e.g., more flexible working conditions).

Follow Up

In Writing: After the meeting, send a thank-you email summarizing your discussion and any agreed-upon next steps. This ensures both parties have a record of the conversation.

Get a Salary Increase - Promotion or Career Advancement

Most companies are constantly looking to promote ambitious and high-performing employees from within. If that sounds like you, climbing the corporate ladder can prove fruitful.

Career advancement encompasses exceptional performance, visibility, continuous learning, networking, and navigating company politics. Moreover, there must be an open position for you to fill unless you can persuade others that a new position should be created to deliver value to the business.

Here are some things to consider concerning career advancement.

Look into the qualifications needed for the next level. This might involve job descriptions, competency frameworks, or discussions with human resources.

Consistently exceed expectations in your current position. Quality work that goes beyond what's asked can set you apart.

Show initiative by identifying and solving problems. Being seen as a problem-solver can mark you as leadership material.

Regularly ask for feedback from your manager and peers to identify areas for improvement and work on them diligently.

Engage in learning opportunities through formal education, online courses, workshops, or certifications relevant to your desired role.

Volunteer for projects critical to the team or company's success, especially those that expose you to other departments or senior management.

Build relationships within and outside your department. Attend company events and join cross-functional teams or committees to expand your internal network.

You don't need a managerial title to demonstrate leadership. Mentor junior colleagues, lead projects, or take charge of meetings to showcase your leadership capabilities.

Bring new ideas to the table. Innovations that improve processes, reduce costs, or generate revenue can significantly boost your promotion prospects.

Let your manager know you're interested in advancing. Discuss your career aspirations clearly and openly and ask for their support.

Work with your manager to create a career development plan that includes short-term goals, learning opportunities, and potential projects aligning with your career aspirations.

Find a mentor within the company for guidance, feedback, and support as you navigate your career path. Similarly, sponsors are influential individuals who can advocate for your promotion. Cultivate relationships with potential sponsors by demonstrating your value and potential.

Understand that many factors influence promotions, including business needs, budget constraints, and internal policies. Be patient, but stay focused on your desires.

Regularly review your career plan, update your skills, and seek new challenges. If a promotion isn't possible in your current organization, it might be time to consider external opportunities.

Start aligning your behavior, work ethic, and attire with the role you're aiming for. "Dress for the job you want, not the job you have" can apply to more than just your wardrobe.

Align your work and contributions with the strategic goals of your team and the organization. Understanding the bigger picture can set you apart as a candidate for advancement.

Maintain an up-to-date list of accomplishments, including metrics, feedback, and recognitions. This will be invaluable in performance reviews and discussions about your career progression.

Finally, career advancement is a marathon, not a sprint, requiring continuous effort, adaptability, and sometimes patience.

Switch Companies or Industries

Switching companies or industries to increase your salary can be a strategic move to boost your earning potential and career trajectory. Also, with job security and career employment at one company being past norms, people constantly switch to better their financial and lifestyle prospects.

First, take stock to understand your current compensation, including salary, bonuses, benefits, and perks. Next, assess the potential for career advancement and salary increases within your current company if it's somewhere you want to stay. If not, consider the following activities for a successful transition.

Research salary benchmarks for your current industry and role. This will give you a baseline for comparison. Investigate salary ranges in the industries you are considering. Some industries may offer higher compensation for similar roles.

Assess the demand for your skills in the job market. Industries with high demand for specific skills may offer more competitive salaries.

Exploring other industries, assessing their salary ranges while considering the cost of living in prospective locations, and researching job market conditions contribute to a comprehensive understanding of potential salary opportunities.

Consider the potential for career advancement and professional development in the new industry. Some industries may provide more rapid advancement opportunities.

Networking and industry research, connecting with professionals in the desired field, and evaluating the company's reputation for financial stability and performance are essential steps. Assess the work culture, values, and reputation of potential employers. A positive work environment can enhance your overall job satisfaction. For example, what are employees saying about the company on Glassdoor?

Review the financial stability and performance of the companies you're considering if data is available. A stable and prosperous company may be more likely to offer competitive salaries.

Additionally, it's essential to consider the transferability of your skills, negotiate effectively during the job offer process, and ensure that the new role aligns with long-term career goals and values. Planning for potential challenges, such as a learning curve or networking adjustments, and reviewing legal considerations, such as non-compete clauses, are crucial for a successful transition.

Interview and Negotiate

Armed with your research, arrange interviews and confidently negotiate your salary during the job offer process. Be prepared to discuss your achievements and the value you bring to the new role. Don't focus solely on base salary.

Consider bonuses, stock options, and other forms of compensation in your negotiations.

Be prepared for a learning curve when entering a new industry. Show your willingness and ability to adapt quickly.

Consider any potential income gaps during the transition period. Have a financial plan in place to cover any temporary financial adjustments.

Get a Side Job

A side or part-time job to complement your existing job can be a fast way to increase your income, and you would be surprised how working an extra eight to sixteen hours weekly can positively impact your cash flow. Employment will guarantee additional wages, whereas self-employment may or may not produce desirable results. Since this book focuses on ending paycheck shortfalls, I recommend the employment option to secure extra cash.

How much additional money do you need? Review your budget and forecast income and expenses when you're considering jobs. For example, you'll have to spend an extra $30 weekly to commute to your new job.

Before pursuing a side job, it's essential to consider several factors. Firstly, ensure that your current employment contract allows additional work outside your primary job. Some companies have policies or clauses restricting employees from engaging in outside employment, so reviewing your employment agreement is crucial.

Once you've confirmed the permissibility of a side job, assess the time commitment required for both positions to ensure you can manage the workload effectively. Striking a balance between your primary job and the side job is essential to prevent burnout and maintain overall job performance.

Consider the nature of the side job and whether it aligns with your skills, interests, and career goals. Ideally, the side job should complement your primary role or provide an opportunity to develop additional skills. Financially, weigh the potential benefits of the side job against the time and energy invested.

Whether seeking extra income, skill development, or pursuing a passion, clearly understanding your objectives will help you choose a side job that aligns with your talents.

At your discretion, inform both employers about your dual employment to maintain transparency and manage expectations regarding your availability. Be mindful of potential conflicts of interest and confidentiality issues, especially if the side job is in a similar industry or involves sensitive information. Discussing these concerns with employers and ensuring compliance with relevant policies might be in your best interest.

Searching for part-time work is the same as hunting for full-time work. Therefore, monitor websites like LinkedIn, Indeed, Monster, etc. Search locally for jobs in your newspaper and on job boards at grocery stores and community centers. Lastly, talk to your network or people in your surrounding area. Not all jobs are advertised, and they might be looking for assistance. For example, some seniors may desire part-time help with grocery shopping, cleaning, or gardening.

Learn and Monetize New Skills

When did you last learn something new or develop a new skill? Central to all these methods of increasing your income is making yourself more valuable to your employer and the world. One way to improve your value is with education, which frequently divides the rich from the poor.

E-learning and online courses are ubiquitous and can be accessed for free or at a low fee. So, it's a convenient way to learn, no matter your schedule or budget. Furthermore, employers love to hear from someone who enjoys and appreciates learning to deliver more value and insights to the organization. Education is sexy and music to their ears.

Consider what courses or specializations might support a raise, promotion, switch, or part-time job. For instance, a digital marketer might benefit from taking courses about search engine marketing, while a customer service representative may benefit from taking sales classes. Your learning plan should align with your career goals to maximize the monetization of your new skills. If you have a job you are targeting, review several like it to understand standard educational and skill requirements.

You'll find reputable courses, specializations, and certifications at Coursera, edX, and HubSpot Academy.

Beware of Scams

Millions of people get conned through scams and promises that never materialize when trying to make more money. Fraudsters promote anything from get-rich-quick business ventures to Ponzi schemes involving fake investment returns. For example, Canada's "Crypto King," Aiden Pleterski, stands accused of conning clients for $30 million. He promoted his trading abilities and above-average returns, only for investors to lose everything.

To protect oneself from scams, it's essential to approach opportunities with a healthy dose of skepticism, conduct thorough research, and be cautious about sharing personal or financial information. Additionally, staying informed about common scams and regularly updating antivirus and anti-malware software can enhance online safety. If something seems too good to be true or raises suspicions, it's advisable to seek advice from trusted sources or authorities before proceeding. Let's review common scams in the landscape.

Pyramid Schemes:
Warning Signs: Promises of quick, exponential returns by recruiting others into the scheme. Lack of a genuine product or service being sold.

Identification: Be wary of opportunities, primarily focusing on recruiting and offering new participants rewards. Legitimate businesses generate revenue through the sale of products or services.

Envelope Stuffing or Assembly Scams:
Warning Signs: Requests for payment upfront in exchange for materials to assemble or products to stuff into envelopes.
Identification: Legitimate work opportunities don't typically require payment upfront. Research the company and look for reviews or complaints from others who may have been scammed.

Online Survey Scams:
Warning Signs: Demands for payment or personal information to access survey opportunities. Unrealistic promises of substantial income.
Identification: Legitimate survey companies don't charge a fee to participate. Be cautious about sharing personal information, and research the company's reputation before getting involved.

Work-from-Home Scams:
Warning Signs: Unsolicited job offers, especially those promising high incomes with little effort. Requests for payment or personal information upfront.
Identification: Legitimate employers do not ask for payment or personal details before hiring. Verify the legitimacy of job offers by researching the company and checking for reviews or testimonials.

Phishing Scams:
Warning Signs: Unsolicited emails, messages, or calls requesting personal or financial information. Urgent or threatening language to create a sense of urgency.
Identification: Legitimate organizations do not ask for sensitive information through unsolicited communications. Verify the organization's legitimacy by contacting the organization directly using official contact information.

Investment Scams:
Warning Signs: Guaranteed high returns with low risk and pressure to invest quickly without proper documentation.

Identification: Be skeptical of investments that seem too good to be true. Verify the legitimacy of investment opportunities by checking with financial regulatory authorities.

Ponzi Schemes

Ponzi schemes are fraudulent investment scams that promise high returns with little risk to investors. They use funds from new investors to pay returns to earlier investors, creating an illusion of profitability. Ponzi schemes can run into the billions, as was the case with Bernie Madoff, the admitted mastermind of the largest known Ponzi scheme in history, worth an estimated $65 billion.

Characteristics of Ponzi Schemes

Consistent, High Returns:
Dealings or Resources: Promises consistently high returns with little or no risk. Legitimate investments carry inherent risks, and consistent, guaranteed high returns are often signs of a Ponzi scheme.

Lack of Transparency:
Dealings or Resources: Limited or no information about the investment strategy, underlying assets, or how returns are generated.

Legitimate investments provide detailed information about the nature of the investment, the associated risks, and the strategy used to generate returns.

Unregistered Investments:
Dealings or Resources: Lack of proper registration with relevant regulatory authorities.
Genuine investment opportunities are typically registered with regulatory bodies. Verify the legitimacy of the investment by checking with financial regulators.

Difficulty in Cash Withdrawals:
Dealings or Resources: Delays or difficulties in withdrawing funds. Promises of better returns for leaving funds invested.
Legitimate investments allow investors to withdraw funds easily. If withdrawals are delayed or discouraged, it could indicate a Ponzi scheme.

Overly Complex Strategies:
Dealings or Resources: Use overly complex investment strategies that are difficult to understand.
Ponzi schemes may use complex jargon or strategies to confuse investors. A lack of transparency in explaining how the returns are generated is a warning sign.

Pressure to Recruit New Investors:
Dealings or Resources: Encouragement or pressure to recruit new investors to join the scheme.
Ponzi schemes rely on new investments to pay returns to existing investors. Pressure to recruit is a common tactic to sustain the scheme.

Inconsistent or Unverifiable Track Record:
Dealings or Resources: Claims of a successful track record without verifiable evidence.
Legitimate investments provide verifiable historical performance data. If a track record is claimed but cannot be verified independently, it raises suspicions.

Promises of Exclusivity:

Dealings or Resources: Promises of exclusive or secret investment opportunities.

Legitimate investments are transparent about their offerings and are accessible to a wide range of investors.

Exercise: Income Boost

We explored a few ways to increase your take-home pay. So, for this exercise, I want you to consider the following questions:

- What method is the most feasible for your situation?
- How long would it take to achieve an income increase?
- What education might you need to support your plans (if any)?
- What would your budget look like if you fulfilled your income goals?

Chapter 8
Rainy Days, Sunny Tomorrows

Life throws unexpected events at us periodically, and some have significant financial repercussions, such as a medical emergency or job layoff. While preparing and expecting unplanned adversity should be standard, many of us are ill-prepared when challenging events occur. Furthermore, these hardships can force us into paycheck hell and keep people there for years.

The chapter covers savings and safeguarding yourself from life's unfortunate surprises.

Emergency Funds for Rainy Days

An emergency fund is a dedicated savings account set aside to cover unexpected or unplanned expenses, providing a financial safety net during times of crisis. Its primary purpose is to provide a cushion for unforeseen events that could otherwise lead to financial strain or debt.

Benefits

An emergency fund provides financial security by covering unexpected expenses like medical emergencies, car repairs, or home maintenance.

Having a readily available fund helps prevent relying on credit cards or loans when faced with unexpected costs, reducing the risk of accumulating debt.

Knowing that you have a financial cushion provides peace of mind, allowing you to navigate unexpected situations with less stress and worry.

An emergency fund provides flexibility and financial autonomy, allowing you to decide based on long-term goals rather than immediate financial pressures.

In the event of job loss or income reduction, an emergency fund can cover essential living expenses until a new source of income is secured.

How Much to Stash

The ideal amount for an emergency fund can vary based on individual circumstances, but a standard recommendation is to aim for three to six months' living expenses. Consider the following factors when determining the appropriate size of your emergency fund:

1. Calculate your essential monthly living expenses, including housing, utilities, groceries, insurance, and debt payments.
2. Individuals with stable employment may lean towards a smaller emergency fund (e.g., three months). In comparison, those with variable income or in more volatile industries may opt for a larger fund (e.g., six months or more).
3. Consider the number of dependents and family members relying on your income. Larger households or those with dependents may opt for a more substantial emergency fund.
4. Assess the potential types of emergencies you may face. For example, homeowners may need a larger fund to cover unexpected home repairs.
5. Evaluate your health insurance coverage. A robust emergency fund can be particularly crucial for covering out-of-pocket medical expenses.

Get Started

Building an emergency fund is a gradual process; the key is consistency. Even if you can't reach the ideal three to six months immediately, having some savings set aside is better than having none. Over time, your emergency fund will grow and provide the financial resilience needed to navigate unexpected challenges.

Begin by setting achievable savings goals. Consistently saving smaller amounts over time can lead to a significant emergency fund accumulation.

Set up automatic transfers from your checking account to your designated emergency fund. This ensures consistent contributions without relying on manual efforts.

Allocate unexpected windfalls, such as tax refunds or work bonuses, toward your emergency fund to expedite growth.

Periodically reassess your financial situation and adjust your emergency fund target as needed. Changes in income, expenses, or family circumstances may warrant adjustments.

Treat building your emergency fund as a financial priority. Consider it an essential step before focusing on other financial objectives, such as investing or discretionary spending.

Pay Day Loans

Payday loans are a standard option for those without emergency funds. A payday loan is a short-term, high-cost loan designed to provide quick access to cash for individuals facing immediate financial needs. These loans are typically small-dollar amounts, and borrowers are expected to repay the loan, along with fees and interest, by their next payday. Payday loans are known for their quick approval process, often requiring minimal documentation and credit checks. Here's how a typical payday loan works:

- Application: Borrowers fill out a loan application, usually providing proof of income, employment, and personal information.
- Approval: Payday lenders typically approve loans quickly, often within minutes, and the borrower receives the funds on the same day.
- Repayment: The borrower is expected to repay the loan in full, including fees and interest, by their next payday. Some lenders may offer the option to extend the loan by paying additional fees.
- Fees and Interest: Payday loans have high costs and annual percentage rates (APRs). The fees are often a fixed amount per $100 borrowed, and the APRs can be extremely high, sometimes reaching triple digits.

Payday loans come with exorbitant interest rates and fees, trapping borrowers in a cycle of borrowing and repaying that can quickly become unsustainable. Instead of relying on payday loans for emergency funds, consider building an emergency savings fund over time. Even small contributions to this fund can add up and provide a financial cushion when unexpected expenses arise. Additionally, exploring alternatives such as credit union loans, personal loans with lower APRs, or even borrowing from friends or family in a pinch can be far more cost-effective and less damaging to your financial future. Educating oneself on the actual cost of payday loans and seeking more sustainable financial solutions can save money and stress in the long run.

Savings for Sunny Tomorrows

Savings involve setting aside a portion of your income for future needs, emergencies, and opportunities. For example, Tyler is saving for his next school semester.

Savings often refer to money that is highly liquid and easily accessible. By contrast, money tied up in stocks, bonds, or commodities may take a few days to access and may be subject to losses, depending on market conditions. Think of savings as money for emergencies and short-term needs. By contrast, investments, real estate, and retirement accounts typically serve long-term goals.

Many benefits of having an emergency fund apply to savings, like financial security and peace of mind.

Options for Short-Term Savings

Savings Accounts
What: Banks and credit unions offer traditional savings accounts.
Advantages: Easy access to funds, low risk, and often comes with interest.
Considerations: Interest rates may be lower compared to other options.

High-Yield Savings Accounts
What: Specialized savings accounts that offer higher interest rates than traditional savings accounts.
Advantages: Higher interest earnings and easy access to funds.
Considerations: Some accounts may have minimum balance requirements.

Certificates of Deposit
What: Time deposits with fixed terms and interest rates.
Advantages: Generally higher interest rates than regular savings accounts, the principal is protected.

Considerations: Limited access to funds until the deposit matures.

Money Market Accounts
What: Accounts that combine features of savings and checking accounts.
Advantages: It may offer higher interest rates and check-writing capabilities.
Considerations: May have minimum balance requirements.

Automated Savings Apps
What: Apps that automate the savings process.
Advantages: Simplifies saving and often incorporates goal-setting features.
Considerations: Check fees and terms associated with specific apps.

Money Market Funds
What: Mutual and exchange-traded funds that invest in money market securities like U.S. treasury bills.
Advantages: A secure, short-term investment option.
Considerations: You'll likely need an investment account to own securities.

Options for Long-Term Savings

Individual Retirement Accounts (IRAs)
Types: Traditional IRA and Roth IRA.
Advantages: Potentially tax-deductible contributions (Traditional IRA) or tax-free withdrawals (Roth IRA) under certain conditions. Flexibility in choosing investments within the IRA.

Employer-Sponsored Retirement Plans
Types: 401(k), 403(b), and 457 plans.
Advantages: Employer contributions and potential matching provide an immediate boost to savings. Tax-deferred growth

on contributions until withdrawal. Automatic payroll deductions for easy contributions.

Health Savings Accounts (HSAs):
Advantages: Triple tax benefits (contributions, growth, and withdrawals for qualified medical expenses are tax-free). It can be used for long-term healthcare expenses in retirement.

Individuals often hold cash, stocks, bonds, and other investments in these accounts.

Exercise: Stress Testing

In finance, a stress test is an analysis or simulation designed to determine the ability of a given financial instrument or financial institution to deal with an economic crisis. For example, JP Morgan Chase can run simulations based on the 2008-09 financial crisis events to understand the strength of its balance sheet and solvency.

An unexpected job loss or health emergency can significantly impact one's finances. So, for this exercise, consider how a job loss, health emergency, home repair, or other material event would impact your budget. Also, consider how you would pay for such events. For example, a dental emergency requires $1,500 to fix. How would you pay for it? Would you cut your discretionary income immediately and borrow the difference to fund the necessary dental procedure?

This exercise recognizes that unplanned events surface and that we should review them beforehand to be somewhat prepared. Alternatively, not planning for surprises or adversity will expose you to financial turmoil.

Chapter 9
30+ Top Money-Saving Tips

There are many ways to save hundreds monthly and thousands annually. I'll share the things I do and my best tips in this chapter. In some cases, the activity will save you a little. In other cases, you'll save a lot. Therefore, adopt the ideas that will serve you the best. Also, brainstorm ideas and improve upon mine to build your savings and wealth faster.

General Tips

    Pay Bills Annually: Opting to pay bills annually instead of monthly is a strategic financial move that can lead to significant savings over time. Many companies, especially those in the streaming and software industries, provide the option for customers to pay for their services annually. By choosing this payment model, subscribers often benefit from substantial discounts, ranging from 10% to 30% or more. While the upfront cost may seem higher, the overall expense is notably lower when compared to monthly payments. This approach not only streamlines budgeting by reducing the frequency of transactions but also translates into considerable savings, allowing individuals to allocate their funds more efficiently.

    Subscribe and Save: Subscribe and Save programs, such as the one offered by Amazon, present a convenient and cost-effective way for customers to manage recurring purchases. By subscribing to regular deliveries of essential items, individuals enjoy the convenience of having products delivered directly to their doorstep and benefit from discounted prices. This service is advantageous for regularly used items like toiletries, household supplies, or pantry staples. The subscription model ensures a steady supply of necessities without the need for repetitive manual orders, streamlining the shopping process. Furthermore, the cost savings associated with Subscribe and Save contribute to a more budget-conscious approach, allowing customers to allocate their funds efficiently and avoid the hassle of last-minute runs to the store.

Bundle Services: Bundling services from telecommunications companies like AT&T and Verizon can be a cost-effective strategy for saving money. By combining wireless, internet, phone, and TV services, these providers often offer bundled deals with significant discounts compared to subscribing to each service individually. However, it's crucial to approach bundles carefully, considering one's needs. While the potential savings are attractive, switching to a bundle is counterproductive if you won't fully utilize the additional services included. Opting for a bundle without a genuine need for all the bundled services might result in unnecessary expenses. Therefore, consumers should carefully evaluate their usage patterns and preferences before committing to a bundled package to ensure that the cost savings align with their specific requirements.

Review Current Plans: Service providers frequently update and reconfigure their offerings to attract new customers, introducing more competitive plans and packages with better terms or pricing. However, existing customers might not be automatically notified about these more advantageous deals. By taking the initiative to review the current plans available annually, you can discover opportunities to reduce your monthly expenses. This proactive approach ensures that you are not missing out on potential savings by sticking with outdated or overpriced plans. It's a simple yet effective way to ensure you get the best service value, potentially freeing up funds for other financial goals or necessities.

Capitalize on Excellent Discounts: To personalize the definition of an "excellent" discount, setting a baseline such as 20% or a minimum of $1 ensures a consistent and measurable threshold for deciding on purchases. When the savings meet or exceed this baseline, the opportunity to stock up on items, like buying two or more of a product, such as cereal or tomato sauce, becomes a financially sound decision. However, it's crucial to maintain budgetary discipline, and if your financial constraints are tight, adjusting the shopping list by removing non-essential items becomes a necessary step.

Change Stores or Providers: Conducting market research and comparison shopping for groceries and services, both online and in-store, provides valuable insights into potential cost savings. Individuals can identify more budget-friendly options by exploring different retailers and providers without compromising quality. Whether it's groceries, insurance, or other essential services, regularly reassessing available choices ensures you are not overpaying for products or services that might be more affordable elsewhere. This strategic shift allows for informed decision-making, empowering individuals to allocate their funds more efficiently and take advantage of the most cost-effective options in the market.

Buy Used: Whether furniture, clothing, electronics or even vehicles, the second-hand market offers many cost-effective options. Buying used allows consumers to access quality products at a fraction of the price they would pay for brand-new equivalents. Thrift stores, online marketplaces, and community platforms provide a diverse selection of pre-owned items in good condition. This approach reduces the strain on your wallet and promotes sustainability by extending the lifespan of goods and minimizing waste.

Swap and Trade: Individuals can trade goods or services with others instead of purchasing new items, creating a mutually beneficial exchange. Online platforms, local community groups, or organized swap events facilitate this process, allowing people to share items they no longer need in exchange for something they require. Swapping can encompass various items, from clothing and household goods to books and toys. This approach helps individuals save money and promotes a culture of reuse, reducing the demand for new products and minimizing environmental impact.

Don't Waste Energy: This should be a standard activity to lower bills, yet many people fall into habits that increase utility costs, such as leaving lights on, taking extended showers, or leaving taps running. Increasing discipline and awareness around energy consumption is crucial to save money on utilities. Simple changes in daily behavior can lead to significant savings. For example, turning off lights when leaving a room, taking shorter showers, fixing leaky faucets promptly, and using energy-efficient appliances can reduce your monthly utility bills. Additionally, considering the installation of low-flow showerheads and LED lightbulbs can further enhance energy savings. You might also use more natural light by opening curtains to save on electricity.

Coupon Websites and Browser Extensions: Coupon websites and browser extensions are potent tools for savvy shoppers looking to stretch their budgets. Numerous online platforms, such as RetailMeNot, Honey, and CouponCabin, are dedicated to aggregating and providing various coupons and promo codes. Incorporating these tools into your online shopping routine can result in substantial savings on multiple products and services. Before making any online purchase, it's wise to check these websites or utilize browser extensions that automatically find and apply relevant codes during checkout.

Grocery and Household Tips

Stick to Your List: A carefully curated shopping list helps you focus on essential items and prevents impulsive purchases that can strain your budget. Before heading to the store, identify your needs, plan meals, and create a list based on these requirements. By adhering strictly to the list while shopping, you avoid the temptation of adding non-essential items to your cart. This disciplined approach prevents overspending and ensures that you make intentional and cost-effective choices. Many excellent shopping apps are available for free.

Review Weekly Specials: Many retailers and supermarkets offer weekly specials featuring discounted prices on various products. Regularly checking these promotions through online circulars, mobile apps, or in-store signage allows you to plan your shopping around the best deals. This will enable you to take advantage of lowered prices on needed items, potentially saving significantly over time. Creating a habit of reviewing weekly specials also promotes mindful spending, helping you make informed choices and allocate your budget more efficiently. It's a small but effective step toward optimizing your shopping experience and maximizing your savings.

Private Label or Generic Products: By forgetting brands and opting for private labels or generic products, consumers can execute a thoughtful and budget-friendly approach to shopping. Retailers like Costco, with their Kirkland label, provide high-quality alternatives to well-known brands at a fraction of the cost. Many other stores offer private labels or generic versions across various products, from groceries to household items. The essential advantage lies in the lower price point, as these products don't carry the brand premium or marketing expenses associated with established names. While the packaging may differ, the quality and ingredients of private-label or generic items are often on par with or even comparable to their brand-name counterparts. This strategy allows individuals to make cost-effective choices without sacrificing quality, ensuring that each purchase meets their budgetary targets.

Shop at Dollar Stores: Dollar stores typically offer various everyday items at significantly lower prices than larger retail chains. You can capitalize on substantial savings by exploring dollar stores for household essentials, cleaning supplies, toiletries, and groceries. While the product selection may vary, dollar stores often provide good value for money, allowing you to stretch your budget further. It's essential to compare prices and quality to ensure the items meet your standards. However, incorporating dollar store shopping into your routine can offer financial gains.

Shop at Bulk Food Stores: These stores allow customers to purchase food items in larger quantities, reducing the per-unit cost. Buying in bulk, you can often take advantage of lower prices for staples like grains, legumes, nuts, and dried fruits. Additionally, many bulk food stores offer a variety of products, including spices, snacks, and even cleaning supplies, enabling you to stock up on essentials at a lower overall expense. While the initial investment might seem higher, the long-term savings and reduced packaging waste make bulk shopping a financially and environmentally conscious choice.

Larger Quantities: Buying larger quantities, such as opting for a larger toothpaste tube, is intelligent and cost-effective. Larger sizes reduce the frequency of repurchasing and offer better value for your money. This approach extends beyond toothpaste to various products like cleaning supplies, pantry staples, and toiletries. However, it's important to consider storage space and product shelf life to ensure practicality.

Exclusive Online Deals: Seizing exclusive online deals is a strategic way to save money while accessing unique offers that may not be available in physical stores. Retailers often use online promotions to sell excess stock or incentivize customers to shop through digital platforms. By taking advantage of these exclusive online deals, consumers can enjoy significant discounts, special promotions, or access to limited-edition products that may not be found in brick-and-mortar stores. This approach allows for cost savings and opens opportunities to explore a broader range of products and discover hidden gems specifically curated for online shoppers. Embracing exclusive online deals is a bright and convenient way to stretch your budget further while enjoying the convenience of virtual shopping.

Post-Holiday Discounts: Buying holiday and seasonal goods after the event has passed will save you money. Retailers often heavily discount these items to clear inventory and make room for other merchandise. Whether it's Christmas lights, Halloween costumes, or festive confectionery, purchasing these items, post-event allows you to take advantage of significant markdowns, like up to 90%. While you won't be able to use some items immediately, planning for the next year can lead to substantial savings. However, product availability can be hit or miss. So, waiting to buy a specific item might not work in your favor because heavily discounted items sell fast.

Make Fewer Shopping Trips: Each trip to the store presents opportunities for impulse purchases, unnecessary spending, and transportation costs like gas or bus fare. By planning and consolidating your shopping, whether for groceries, household items, or other necessities, you reduce the frequency of these opportunities.

Get Every Last Drop: Getting every drop out of household items is a small yet impactful way to save money and reduce waste. Squeezing the last bit of toothpaste or using every drop of laundry detergent ensures you maximize the value of the products you purchase. This practice extends beyond toothpaste and detergent; it applies to cosmetics, condiments, and other household items. By being mindful of how we use these products and finding creative ways to utilize every last bit, we save money in the long run and contribute to a more sustainable and eco-friendly lifestyle. It's a simple habit that aligns with financial prudence and responsible consumption, emphasizing the importance of minimizing waste daily.

Eat Smaller Portions: By being mindful of portion sizes, individuals can reduce food expenses while meeting their nutritional needs. Opting for smaller servings not only cuts down on grocery costs but also minimizes food waste. Planning meals, using smaller plates, and savoring each bite can help control portion sizes and foster a healthier relationship with food. Additionally, incorporating more whole foods, such as fruits, vegetables, and grains, into meals can be a budget-friendly and nutritious way to manage portion control.

Clothing Tips

Extend Wearability: Rather than replacing clothing annually, consider adopting a more frugal approach by wearing your clothes for an additional six months to a year. Before making new purchases, evaluate the condition of your existing wardrobe and identify items that still serve their purpose. Then, donating clothes that are still wearable to thrift stores is an excellent practice, contributing to sustainability while making room for new additions. Maintaining a spreadsheet to list and date fashion purchases can be valuable for making informed replacement decisions. This thoughtful and intentional approach to wardrobe management ensures that every clothing purchase aligns with your budgetary goals and reduces unnecessary spending on items with significant wear left.

Buy During Seasonal Clearouts: Retailers need to keep their inventory current to align with the latest fashion trends, leading them to offer substantial discounts on last season's merchandise to free up space for new arrivals. For example, as summer transitions to fall, you'll find summer clothing at deeply discounted prices to make room for fall and winter collections. These clearance sales often occur within a defined two-week period, offering "blowout" prices to quickly move remaining stock. While the available sizes and styles might be limited due to the clearance nature of these sales, strategic timing, and prompt shopping can lead to fantastic deals on high-quality items. To make the most of these opportunities, it's beneficial to keep an eye on your favorite stores' sale schedules and be ready to shop as soon as the clearouts begin. This approach helps stretch your clothing budget further and allows you to acquire pieces from premium brands at a fraction of the cost.

Banking Tips

Avoid Overdraft Fees: Overdraft fees occur when account balances fall below zero, triggering additional charges for each transaction made in this state. To steer clear of these costly fees ($20 to $40 per overdraft), it's essential to keep a close eye on your account balance, set up low-balance alerts, and practice responsible budgeting. Budgeting tools or apps can help you track your spending and ensure you don't overspend.

Avoid Cash Advances: Cash advances often come with high fees and interest rates, making them an expensive way to access funds. Credit card companies typically charge a fee for cash advances, a percentage of the amount withdrawn. Additionally, interest accrues immediately, without the usual grace period for regular credit card purchases. Individuals can sidestep these costly charges and the potential for accumulating high-interest debt by steering clear of cash advances. It's advisable to explore alternative methods of obtaining funds, such as using a debit card for purchases or withdrawing cash from an ATM with a checking account, to ensure a more cost-effective approach to managing finances.

Maintain a Minimum Balance: Some banks reward customers who keep minimum balances. For example, they may waive monthly maintenance fees, offer higher interest rates on savings accounts, or provide free checking accounts. By maintaining the required minimum balance, you can avoid unnecessary fees and earn more through higher interest rates, saving money over time. This strategy requires discipline and a good understanding of your monthly cash flow to ensure the balance does not fall below the minimum necessary. Still, it can lead to significant savings and benefits that enhance your financial health.

Other Tips

Discuss Money-Saving Tips: Asking for and sharing savings tips with friends creates a collaborative approach to frugality, fostering a community of financial mindfulness. By openly discussing money-saving strategies, you can discover new ideas and perspectives that might not have occurred to you individually. Sharing insights on budgeting, finding deals, or cost-effective habits can empower everyone involved to make smarter financial choices. Additionally, this collaborative effort extends beyond savings tips, potentially leading to group activities or initiatives that promote cost-conscious living. Cultivating an open dialogue about finances among friends strengthens relationships and creates a supportive environment for achieving shared financial goals.

Declutter and Sell Stuff: You'll free up physical space and generate extra cash by decluttering your space and selling unwanted belongings through online marketplaces or garage sales. Rather than letting unused items accumulate, you can convert them into funds that contribute directly to your budget. This approach aligns with a minimalist lifestyle, emphasizing quality over quantity. The money earned from selling can be earmarked for specific purposes, whether funding future purchases, building an emergency fund, or paying off debts.

Find Cheaper Entertainment: Instead of splurging on expensive outings or activities, explore budget-friendly alternatives that still offer fulfillment. Look for community events, free concerts, or outdoor activities, which often provide entertainment at little to no cost. Subscription services for streaming movies or online platforms for gaming can also offer affordable options for home-based leisure. Additionally, consider utilizing local libraries for books and DVDs or attending free workshops or lectures. By being creative and open to exploring less expensive entertainment avenues, you can significantly reduce discretionary spending while having fulfilling experiences. This approach supports financial goals and encourages a more mindful and intentional approach to leisure activities.

Do-It-Yourself: Embracing a do-it-yourself (DIY) mindset is a powerful and money-saving approach across various aspects of life. Whether home improvement, crafting, or even basic repairs, tackling tasks yourself can lead to substantial savings. DIY projects eliminate the need for professional services and empower individuals to learn new skills and gain a sense of accomplishment. From minor repairs around the house to creating homemade gifts, the DIY approach minimizes labor costs and allows you to tailor projects to your budget. Online tutorials, instructional videos, and community forums provide valuable resources for honing your DIY skills. By taking the initiative to handle tasks independently, you save money and cultivate a sense of self-reliance and creativity, making DIY an enriching and cost-effective lifestyle choice.

Hire Students: Students often bring enthusiasm, fresh perspectives, and a willingness to learn. Additionally, their hourly rates or project fees may be more budget-friendly than hiring experienced professionals. Whether it's assistance with research, social media management, graphic design, or other projects, tapping into the student workforce can lead to significant cost savings for businesses or individuals. Establishing clear expectations and communication channels and providing guidance is essential for a successful collaboration.

Work Remotely: The elimination of daily commutes not only reduces transportation costs but also results in savings on fuel or public transit expenses. Remote work often has a more relaxed dress code, allowing individuals to curtail spending on professional wardrobes. Another notable advantage is the potential reduction in lunch expenses, as preparing meals at home tends to be more cost-effective than dining out. Beyond these immediate savings, remote work can improve work-life balance, potentially reducing stress and enhancing overall well-being.

Tire Pressure: Maintaining proper tire pressure is a simple yet effective way to save money and promote vehicle longevity. Adequate tire pressure not only enhances fuel efficiency but also extends the lifespan of your tires. Underinflated tires can increase rolling resistance, forcing the engine to work harder and consume more fuel. This, in turn, leads to higher fuel expenses. Moreover, properly inflated tires are worn more evenly, reducing the frequency of tire replacements and saving on maintenance costs.

Explore Transportation Options: Rather than defaulting to a personal vehicle for daily travel or work, explore alternative modes of transportation, including public transit, cycling, walking, or carpooling. Public transportation often proves to be a more cost-effective choice, eliminating fuel, parking, and maintenance expenses associated with private vehicles. Cycling and walking not only save on transportation costs but also contribute to improved health and well-being. Carpooling or ride sharing with colleagues or neighbors allows for cost-sharing and reduces the environmental impact of individual commuting.

Chapter 10
MONEY MINDSET MAKEOVER

Financial success isn't only about numbers and math; there's a psychological component to efficient money management. Understanding your attitudes, beliefs, and behaviors surrounding money is just as crucial as mastering budgeting or investment strategies. The psychological aspect involves recognizing emotional triggers related to spending, identifying limiting beliefs about wealth, and cultivating a positive mindset toward financial goals. By addressing these psychological elements, you gain control over impulsive financial decisions and foster a healthier relationship with money, paving the way for sustained economic success and wellness.

This chapter reviews money psychology, personal transformation, and engaging with family members.

Mind Over Money

Make Money Your Friend

The "Make Money Your Friend" concept revolves around shifting one's perspective from viewing money solely as a means of survival or a source of stress to seeing it as a valuable ally. This approach encourages individuals to foster a positive relationship with their finances, recognizing money's potential to enable personal growth, provide security, and open doors to opportunities. Also, embracing money as a friend means understanding and respecting its value, learning how to manage it wisely, and using it to align with one's values and goals. It involves moving beyond the fear and anxiety surrounding financial matters and adopting a mindset of abundance and possibility. By doing so, individuals can break free from limiting beliefs that hinder their financial progress and start making more informed, empowered decisions. Making money your friend is about accumulating wealth and developing a healthy, balanced, and proactive relationship with finances to support a fulfilling and prosperous life.

Your Money Mindset

Embarking on a journey to transform your money mindset is a powerful and reflective endeavor. Start by taking a moment to reflect on your beliefs, attitudes, and money-related behaviors. This self-awareness is the first step toward initiating positive change in your financial life.

Consider your upbringing, past experiences, and cultural influences that may have shaped your views on money. How do you feel about wealth, success, and financial security? Are there specific emotions or memories tied to your financial decisions? Understanding these aspects provides valuable insights into the roots of your current mindset.

Identifying any limiting beliefs or negative thought patterns that might be acting as barriers to your financial growth is essential. These could be thoughts like "I'm not good with money" or "I'll never be able to save enough." Pinpointing these beliefs allows you to confront and challenge them.

Ask yourself: What stories or narratives have you been telling yourself about money? Are there recurring patterns in your financial behavior holding you back? Perhaps you've internalized societal expectations or inherited limiting beliefs from family and friends. Identifying these patterns empowers you to break free from their constraints.

The purpose of this reflection is not to judge or criticize but to understand and grow. Recognize that everyone has areas where they can improve and evolve, and your willingness to explore your money mindset is a commendable first step toward positive change.

As you delve into this process, be patient and compassionate with yourself. Transforming your money mindset is a journey, not a destination. By clarifying your beliefs and identifying potential roadblocks, you pave the way for a healthier and more empowering relationship with money.

Take this opportunity to envision the financial mindset you aspire to cultivate. What beliefs and attitudes would support your financial goals and well-being? Use this reflection as a foundation for the positive changes you aim to make toward financial growth and fulfillment.

Experiences and Values

People's attitudes toward money are intricately woven with their life experiences and values, creating a unique financial mindset shaped by various factors.

Childhood plays a pivotal role, with the financial atmosphere at home influencing early perceptions of money management.

Educational background contributes significantly, with financial education impacting attitudes toward budgeting, investing, and overall financial literacy. Cultural and societal influences, including expectations and norms related to spending and saving, further shape individual financial perspectives.

Personal financial experiences, whether marked by success or setbacks, leave lasting imprints that influence risk-taking tendencies or a preference for financial caution. Peer influence and societal comparisons impact spending habits, as individuals may strive to align with external expectations.

Life events, especially those marked by trauma or significant change, can profoundly alter financial attitudes, fostering a heightened focus on security or risk aversion. Personal values and priorities, such as the importance of family, experiences, or philanthropy, guide financial decisions, influencing how people allocate their resources.

By recognizing the interplay between experiences and values, individuals can gain insight into their financial attitudes and make intentional choices aligned with their unique perspectives and long-term plans.

Myths and Misconceptions

By confronting common myths and reevaluating your beliefs about money, you can adopt a more positive and empowering financial mindset. This transformation enhances your relationship with money and supports your overall journey toward financial success and personal fulfillment. Here are four common myths:

- Wealth Equals Happiness: One of the most pervasive myths is that acquiring wealth automatically leads to happiness. While financial stability can relieve stress related to financial insecurity, happiness is influenced by various factors, including relationships, personal fulfillment, health, and more. Wealth can provide opportunities and comfort, but it's not a guaranteed source of happiness.
- You Must Be Born Into Money to Be Wealthy: This myth perpetuates the belief that wealth and success are exclusive to those who inherit them. However, countless stories of self-made individuals prove that achieving significant financial success through hard work, innovation, and perseverance is possible, regardless of one's starting point.
- Investing Is Only for the Rich: Many believe investing is a complex and inaccessible world reserved for those already wealthy. Technological advancements and financial education have made investing more accessible than ever. With the advent of micro-investing apps and platforms, individuals can start investing with small amounts of money.
- Debt Is Always Bad: While excessive debt can be harmful, not all debt is negative. Strategic borrowing, such as student loans for education or mortgages for home ownership, can be considered investments in your future. The key is to manage debt wisely and ensure it aligns with your long-term aspirations.

Negative or Limiting Beliefs

Begin by writing down your beliefs about money, wealth, and success. Recognize which of these are negative or limiting. Acknowledging these beliefs is the first step in challenging them.

For every limiting belief, look for evidence that contradicts it. If you believe you cannot achieve wealth because of your background, research stories of individuals who have succeeded despite similar or more significant challenges.

Once you've identified and challenged your limiting beliefs, work on reframing them into positive affirmations. For example, change "I'll never be good with money" to "I am capable of learning and improving my financial management skills."

Knowledge is a powerful tool for overcoming misconceptions. Invest time in financial education through books, courses, podcasts, and seminars. Understanding the basics of personal finance, investing, and wealth-building can demystify many misconceptions and empower you to make informed decisions.

Your environment and network can significantly influence your beliefs and attitudes towards money. Surround yourself with individuals who have a healthy relationship with money and success. Engage in communities that support financial literacy and personal growth.

Focusing on what you have rather than your deficiencies can shift your perspective on wealth and success. Practicing gratitude and mindfulness helps you appreciate the abundance in your life, reducing the negative emotions tied to financial goals.

Transformation and Growth

Cultivate a Positive Money Mindset

How we perceive and approach our financial journey significantly influences the outcomes we experience. An optimistic mindset enhances our resilience in the face of challenges, attracts opportunities, and encourages proactive decision-making. Embracing a positive mindset involves recognizing and appreciating the abundance in our lives. Instead of focusing on scarcity or what may be lacking, it entails acknowledging the resources, opportunities, and strengths at our disposal. This shift in perspective lays the foundation for a more open and constructive approach to financial planning.

Mindset-shifting practices play a crucial role in fostering this positive outlook. Gratitude, as a practice, involves intentionally acknowledging and appreciating the positive aspects of our lives, including our financial circumstances. Regularly expressing gratitude for economic stability, opportunities, and supportive relationships can reshape our perspective on wealth. Visualization is another powerful tool where individuals mentally picture their desired financial future. This practice helps create a vivid image of success, reinforcing the belief that such outcomes are attainable. Affirmations, or positive statements repeated consistently, contribute to rewiring our thought patterns. By affirming our ability to achieve financial goals and maintain a healthy relationship with money, we reinforce positive beliefs and reduce self-limiting thoughts.

These mindset-shifting practices are not merely positive thinking exercises but practical tools that influence our behaviors and decisions. As we incorporate gratitude, visualization, and affirmations into our daily routines, we create a positive feedback loop that aligns our thoughts, emotions, and actions with our financial aspirations. Fostering a positive and abundance-oriented mindset is not just about wishful thinking; it's about adopting a proactive and empowered approach to our financial journey, maximizing our potential for success and satisfaction.

Build Good Habits

Rather than fixating solely on achieving specific financial goals, cultivating habits such as budgeting, saving, and wise spending promotes a holistic and adaptive approach to financial happiness. Good habits form the backbone of consistent and responsible financial behavior, providing a framework that can withstand the unpredictability of life.

Individuals develop a mindset that prioritizes financial discipline, resilience, and adaptability by concentrating on habits. This emphasis on habits acknowledges that financial success is a journey, and the cumulative impact of consistent positive behaviors is more influential than fixating on isolated achievements. Furthermore, building good financial habits fosters a proactive and mindful relationship with money, empowering individuals to navigate challenges and seize opportunities as they arise, ultimately contributing to a more secure and balanced financial future.

Celebrate Your Victories

In pursuing financial freedom, it's easy to overlook smaller milestones, yet these accomplishments contribute significantly to overall progress. Recognizing and celebrating these victories, whether sticking to a budget, saving a certain amount, or paying off a debt, instills a sense of accomplishment and motivation. Celebrating small wins builds momentum and reinforces the belief that larger goals are achievable.

Equally important is cultivating a mindset of gratitude and contentment amidst the journey toward more substantial financial objectives. While it's natural to aspire to more remarkable financial milestones, practicing gratitude for current financial stability, opportunities, and resources brings a sense of fulfillment. This mindset shift helps counteract the tendency to constantly chase the next goal without appreciating the present. Gratitude fosters contentment, reducing the stress associated with always reaching for more. Balancing the pursuit of ambitious financial goals with gratitude for current blessings creates a harmonious and positive approach to money management. By acknowledging achievements, big and small, and maintaining an attitude of thankfulness, individuals can build a healthier and more sustainable relationship with their finances.

Seek Professional Guidance

One of my goals for writing this book was to give you all the information and tips you need to improve your finances independently. However, "help" isn't a nasty four-letter word. Instead, the proper assistance at an affordable price can accelerate your results.

While managing personal finances independently is valuable, engaging with financial experts adds a layer of knowledge and expertise that can significantly enhance one's financial strategy.

Money coaches, financial planners, advisors, and consultants possess insights into complex financial landscapes, offering tailored advice based on individual circumstances. Whether creating a comprehensive financial plan, optimizing investments, or navigating tax implications, professionals bring a depth of knowledge that can be challenging to attain alone. Their objective perspective can help individuals make informed decisions, especially during significant life events or economic uncertainties. Collaborating with professionals not only provides strategic financial solutions but also fosters a sense of confidence and security in one's financial journey. It's an investment in both present and future financial success, offering personalized guidance to navigate the complexities of the financial world. Let's look more closely at financial professionals and their responsibilities.

Credit Counselor

A credit counselor is a professional who specializes in providing guidance and assistance to individuals facing challenges related to their credit and debt management. These counselors work closely with clients to assess their financial situations, review credit reports, and develop strategies to improve their creditworthiness. Credit counselors may offer advice on budgeting, debt repayment plans, and negotiating with creditors to reduce interest rates or create more manageable payment schedules. They also educate clients on responsible financial behaviors to prevent future credit issues. Many credit counselors work for nonprofit organizations and aim to empower individuals to regain control of their finances and build a more stable future.

Money or Financial Coach

A money coach, often called a financial coach, focuses on guiding individuals in developing a healthy and positive relationship with money. Unlike traditional financial advisors who primarily offer investment advice, money coaches delve into clients' behaviors, beliefs, and attitudes toward money. They help clients identify and overcome emotional and psychological financial barriers, providing practical strategies for budgeting, saving, and achieving financial goals. Money coaches often empower clients to make informed decisions and develop positive financial habits.

Financial Planner

A financial planner is a professional who takes a holistic approach to an individual's financial well-being. They assess various aspects of a client's financial situation, including income, expenses, investments, insurance, and estate planning. Financial planners create comprehensive financial plans that outline specific strategies to help clients achieve their short-term and long-term goals. These professionals may also offer retirement planning, tax management, and risk management guidance to ensure a well-rounded and personalized financial strategy.

Investment Advisor

An investment advisor specializes in providing advice and guidance on investment-related matters. This professional helps clients make informed decisions about allocating their assets, selecting specific investments, and managing their portfolios. Investment advisors stay abreast of market trends, risk factors, and economic conditions to provide tailored recommendations that align with clients' financial objectives. They may work with individuals, families, or institutions to optimize investment returns and mitigate risks. Instead of a human advisor, millions of people use roboadvisers and investment apps to invest in low-cost exchange-traded fund portfolios, for example, Acorns and Betterment.

Tax Accountant

Tax accountants help individuals in navigating the complexities of taxation. These experts focus on various aspects of an individual's financial situation, primarily related to tax preparation and planning. Personal tax accountants work closely with clients to gather financial information, assess eligibility for deductions and credits, and ensure accurate and timely filing of annual tax returns. Beyond tax season, they engage in proactive tax planning, advising clients on strategies to optimize their tax positions and minimize liabilities throughout the year. These professionals stay abreast of changes in tax laws, providing up-to-date guidance to ensure compliance. In the event of audits or inquiries from tax authorities, personal tax accountants act as advocates for their clients, facilitating communication and resolution. Their year-round support addresses client queries, offers advice on financial decisions with tax implications, and assists with estate planning or retirement considerations.

Choosing Financial Professionals

Choosing the right financial professional is a critical decision that can significantly impact your financial matters. Here are some steps to guide you in selecting a financial professional.

Identify your financial needs and objectives. Whether you need help with budgeting, investing, retirement planning, or debt management, understanding your specific requirements will guide your selection.

Familiarize yourself with financial professionals, such as financial advisors, planners, investment advisors, and credit counselors. Each has a distinct focus, and your choice should align with your priorities.

Look for professionals with relevant credentials and qualifications. Certifications like Certified Financial Planner (CFP), Chartered Financial Analyst (CFA), or Certified Public Accountant (CPA) indicate a commitment to professionalism and expertise.

Evaluate the professional's experience in dealing with situations like yours. Ask for references or reviews, and consider how long they've been practicing in the financial industry.

Understand the professional's fee structure. Some charge hourly fees, while others work on a commission or a percentage of assets under management. Ensure transparency in their compensation and that the fee structure aligns with your preferences.

Choose a financial professional with a fiduciary duty, meaning they are legally obligated to act in your best interest. This ensures that their recommendations prioritize your financial well-being.

Pay attention to the communication style of the professional. A good financial advisor should be able to explain complex concepts in a way you understand. Regular communication and updates are essential for a successful partnership.

Consider how accessible the professional is and whether they can accommodate your preferred communication methods. Having a responsive and available advisor is crucial, especially during significant financial decisions or market fluctuations.

Choose someone whose values and approach align with yours. A good fit in terms of personality and communication style can contribute to a more productive and satisfying working relationship.

Don't hesitate to interview multiple candidates. This will give you a better understanding of different approaches and help you make an informed decision.

Research the professional's disciplinary history through regulatory bodies or organizations. This information can provide insights into their ethical conduct.

Family Engagement

Engaging in open and honest conversations about financial matters within your family, especially with a partner or children, is a powerful catalyst for numerous positive outcomes.

Discussing financial matters within a relationship creates a space for emotional connection and understanding. It's an opportunity to share aspirations, concerns, and goals, deepening the bond between partners. As you openly communicate about money, you address financial matters and strengthen your relationship's emotional foundation.

Money can be a significant source of stress in many households. Talking about financial matters allows for a cathartic release of this stress. By voicing concerns, sharing burdens, and collectively problem-solving, you're addressing the practical aspects of financial challenges and alleviating the emotional toll they can take. It transforms financial stress from an isolating burden to a shared responsibility.

For families with children, involving them in financial discussions creates a sense of unity and shared purpose. It fosters an environment where everyone feels part of a team working towards common goals. This unity strengthens family bonds and instills a collective mindset, reinforcing that financial decisions impact the entire family.

Engaging in financial conversations with children invests in their financial literacy and life skills. It gives them real-world education about budgeting, saving, and responsible spending. These discussions lay the groundwork for a healthy relationship with money, preparing them for future financial independence and decision-making.

In a relationship, discussing financial matters ensures that both partners are on the same page regarding their financial goals. It's an opportunity to align visions for the future, whether saving for a home, planning for education, or preparing for retirement. This alignment helps prevent misunderstandings, fosters a sense of shared responsibility, and promotes joint decision-making.

Transparent communication about financial matters establishes a culture of accountability within the family. It encourages everyone to take ownership of their financial roles and responsibilities. Whether adhering to a budget, contributing to savings, or making financial decisions, open discussions create a sense of accountability that strengthens the family's financial health.

In essence, talking about financial matters within your family is not just a pragmatic approach to managing money; it's a holistic strategy that nurtures emotional connection, teaches valuable life skills, and fosters a sense of unity and accountability. It transforms financial discussions from potential sources of tension into opportunities for growth, understanding, and shared success.

Chapter 11
Five-Star Financial Apps

Decades ago, banks and investment firms were almost the sole navigators for people managing their financial matters. The landscape is much different today, with innovative and low-cost alternatives transforming the financial services industry. The rise of fintech companies, online platforms, and robo-advisors has democratized access to financial tools, offering individuals many options beyond traditional banking. This shift empowers consumers to take control of their finances, access a broader range of services, and choose platforms that align with their specific needs and preferences. The evolving financial ecosystem reflects a more inclusive and dynamic approach, giving individuals the flexibility to tailor their financial journey in ways unimaginable in the past.

This chapter reviews top-rated financial apps and tools for education, budgeting, debt reduction, banking, tax prep, and more.

Education

Investopedia is a leading educational platform that offers a comprehensive app for learning about finance and investing. It provides articles, tutorials, and videos covering various financial topics, from basic concepts to advanced investing strategies. Investopedia's app is a valuable resource for individuals looking to enhance their financial knowledge and make informed decisions.

Coursera is a leading online learning platform providing individuals access to diverse, high-quality courses, certifications, and degree programs. Coursera collaborates with renowned universities, institutions, and industry experts worldwide to offer educational content across various disciplines. The platform leverages a mix of video lectures, interactive quizzes, and peer-graded assignments to deliver engaging and effective online education. Coursera's flexibility enables users to learn at their own pace, making it an accessible option for individuals seeking to upskill, reskill, or pursue academic credentials. Visit the site and search "personal finance" for its current offerings.

NerdWallet's app combines educational content with practical tools to help users make informed financial decisions. It offers guides on credit cards, loans, insurance, and investing, along with calculators and comparison tools. NerdWallet's app is user-friendly and provides personalized recommendations based on individual financial goals and preferences, making it a valuable resource for those seeking guidance in various financial areas.

Budgeting

YNAB (You Need A Budget) is a popular budgeting app with a zero-based budgeting philosophy. It helps users allocate every dollar to specific categories, ensuring a purpose for each cent. YNAB offers real-time syncing across devices, goal-setting features, and insightful reports that empower users to take control of their finances. With a user-friendly interface and educational resources, YNAB stands out for its effectiveness in helping individuals and families create and stick to a budget.

PocketGuard is known for its simplicity and intuitive design. It connects to users' financial accounts, categorizes transactions, and displays an overview of spending against income. PocketGuard's standout feature is its "In My Pocket" metric, which shows how much money is available for discretionary spending after bills and savings. With customizable budget categories and goal-setting capabilities, PocketGuard is favored for its straightforward approach to financial management.

Rocket Money offers a personal finance app to help users save money, manage their subscriptions, and stay on top of their bills. The app automatically analyzes user spending habits to identify areas where they may be overspending or forgetting about recurring charges. It also allows users to cancel unwanted subscriptions directly from the app and provides alerts for upcoming bill payments. Additionally, Rocket Money offers an "AutoSave" feature that enables users to set savings goals and automatically transfer funds to a separate account. Rocket Money aims to give users greater visibility into their finances and empower them to make more informed decisions about their spending and saving habits.

Debt Reduction

The Debt Payoff Planner app streamlines the process of managing outstanding debts by allowing users to input detailed information about each debt, including interest rates, minimum payments, and total balances. One of its key features is the ability for users to set personalized financial targets, whether it's a specific payoff date or a preferred debt repayment strategy like the snowball or avalanche method. The app then generates a tailored debt repayment plan, breaking down monthly contributions to each debt account. With visual progress tracking, users can monitor their journey towards becoming debt-free, gaining motivation and clarity on their financial path. Additionally, the Debt Payoff Planner app often includes scenario planning features, enabling users to simulate the impact of extra payments or changes in strategy.

Credit Scores

The Credit Karma app is a comprehensive and user-friendly financial tool that gives individuals insights into their credit health and overall financial well-being. With a clean and intuitive interface, the app allows users to access their credit scores from major credit bureaus, providing a clear snapshot of their creditworthiness. Beyond credit scores, Credit Karma offers detailed credit reports, highlighting factors influencing the scores and giving personalized recommendations for improvement. One standout feature is the app's Credit Monitoring, which alerts users to changes in their credit reports, helping them stay vigilant against potential fraud or errors. Credit Karma provides users with various financial resources, including educational articles, tax preparation tools, and personalized credit card or loan recommendations based on their credit profiles. As a free service, the Credit Karma app empowers users to make informed financial decisions, monitor their credit health, and work towards achieving their financial goals.

    The CreditWise app from Capital One is a free tool designed to help individuals monitor and improve their credit health. Accessible to Capital One customers and the public, the app offers real-time access to your credit score, specifically TransUnion data, a commonly used credit scoring model. Beyond just providing a credit score, CreditWise excels in offering a detailed credit report that helps users understand the factors affecting their score, such as credit utilization, payment history, and recent inquiries. One of its notable features is the Credit Simulator, which allows users to see how certain financial decisions, like paying off debt or opening a new account, might impact their credit score. This proactive approach empowers users to make informed economic choices. Additionally, CreditWise provides personalized tips for improving credit health and alerts users to potential identity fraud by scanning the dark web for their information. You don't have to be a Capital One cardholder to use this tool.

Mobile Banking

Chime is a digital bank offering checking and savings accounts and other financial services such as direct deposit, mobile check deposits, and fee-free overdraft protection. One unique feature of Chime is its "SpotMe" service, which allows eligible customers to overdraw their accounts by up to $100 without incurring fees. Chime's mobile app also includes budgeting tools and automatic savings features, making it easy for users to track their spending and build up their savings balances over time.

Current is another digital banking platform offering teenagers and young adults checking accounts and debit cards. The Current app includes parental controls, real-time transaction notifications, and early access to direct deposit paychecks. Current also offers cash-back rewards at specific merchants and has partnered with companies like Netflix and Spotify to provide discounts on popular streaming services.

Varo is a mobile banking app that provides FDIC-insured checking and savings accounts, budgeting tools, automated savings features, and fee-free overdraft protection. Varo stands out for its high-yield savings account, which frequently is higher than many traditional brick-and-mortar banks. Varo also offers a variety of credit-building products, including a secured credit card and personal loans, making it a good option for individuals looking to improve their credit scores.

Mortgage Rates

Bankrate is a well-established financial website that provides comprehensive information on various financial products, including mortgages. It allows you to compare mortgage rates from different lenders and offers additional tools and resources to help with your decision.

LendingTree is a popular online marketplace that connects borrowers with lenders. It allows you to compare mortgage rates from multiple lenders after filling out a single online form.

LendingTree also provides tools to explore different loan options.

Zillow, known for its real estate listings, offers a mortgage rate comparison tool. It provides a simple interface for comparing rates and exploring different loan options based on your financial situation and preferences.

Credible is an online marketplace that allows you to compare personalized loan offers from various lenders, including mortgage rates. It simplifies the process by presenting multiple loan options in one place.

Investing

Acorns is a micro-investing app that rounds up everyday purchases to the nearest dollar and invests the spare change. It offers a hands-off approach to investing, making it accessible for individuals looking to start with small amounts. Acorns also provides automated portfolio management, educational content, and features like "Found Money," where users can earn cashback for purchases made with partner brands.

Betterment employs a robo-advisor approach to create and manage diversified investment portfolios based on users' financial goals, risk tolerance, and time horizons. Betterment's sophisticated algorithms continuously optimize portfolios, automatically rebalancing and reinvesting dividends to maximize returns. Users benefit from features like goal-based investing, tax-efficient strategies, and automatic deposits. The app's intuitive interface provides clear insights into portfolio performance and progress toward financial objectives. With low fees and a commitment to transparency, Betterment has become popular for those seeking a hands-off yet personalized approach to long-term wealth building.

Vanguard is a well-established investment platform known for its low-cost index funds and commitment to investor interests. The Vanguard app allows users to manage their investment portfolios, access research materials, and execute trades. With a focus on long-term investing and various low-cost fund options, Vanguard appeals to those seeking a reliable and reputable platform for building wealth over time.

Wealthfront is a prominent robo-advisor platform offering a streamlined and tech-driven approach to investment management. Catering to investors looking for a hands-off approach, the app leverages algorithms to construct and optimize diversified portfolios based on individual financial goals, risk tolerance, and time horizons. Wealthfront's unique selling points include tax-loss harvesting, designed to minimize tax liabilities, and direct indexing, which enhances tax efficiency for taxable accounts. The app's Path tool provides comprehensive financial planning, projects future wealth, and offers insights into users' financial journeys. Wealthfront also prioritizes low-cost, commission-free investing, making it an appealing option for those seeking a straightforward yet sophisticated investment solution to grow their wealth over time.

Money Transfer (Local)

PayPal is one of the oldest and most widely used online payment systems, allowing users to send and receive money electronically through its website and mobile app. With PayPal, you can link your bank account, credit card, or debit card to fund transactions and then send money to anyone with an email address or phone number. PayPal also offers buyer and seller protections and business solutions for small businesses and e-commerce sites.

Venmo is a mobile payment service owned by PayPal that allows users to transfer money quickly and easily to friends, family members, and businesses using their smartphones. Venmo uses a social feed to let users see what their contacts are buying and selling, adding a layer of fun and community to the experience. Like PayPal, Venmo supports linked bank accounts, credit cards, and debit cards, allowing users to request and send money with just a few taps.

Cash App, formerly known as Square Cash, is another popular peer-to-peer payment app that lets users send and receive money via their phones. Cash App is known for its simplicity and ease of use, with no need to add contacts or create groups - enter a dollar amount and the recipient's username (known as a "$cashtag") to initiate a transfer. Cash App also allows users to invest in stocks and purchase cryptocurrencies and supports linked bank accounts, credit cards, and debit cards.

Money Transfer (International)

Wise offers international money transfers at mid-market exchange rates with transparent fees. Wise uses a peer-to-peer network to match currency orders and avoid the hidden costs associated with traditional banks and brokers. In addition to international transfers, Wise offers borderless bank accounts with local account numbers in multiple countries, making it easier for freelancers, remote workers, and frequent travelers to manage their finances across borders.

Remitly is a digital remittance service specializing in international money transfers, particularly for immigrants sending money home to their families. Remitly boasts fast delivery times, low fees, and competitive exchange rates and supports transfers to over 150 countries worldwide. Users can choose from several delivery methods, including bank deposits, cash pickups, and mobile wallets, depending on the country they are sending to. Remitly also offers a variety of security measures, such as two-factor authentication and encryption, to protect users' sensitive information.

Revolut offers a range of financial services, including international money transfers. With Revolut, users can hold and convert multiple currencies within the app and send money abroad using the interbank exchange rate with minimal markup. Revolut also offers free international ATM withdrawals, travel insurance, and budgeting tools, among other perks. However, while Revolut's fees can be lower than those of traditional banks, they may still be higher than those of dedicated remittance services like Remitly.

Tax Preparation

By using guided tax preparation software, IRS Free File lets qualified taxpayers prepare and file federal income tax returns online. It's safe, easy, and at no cost to you. Those who don't qualify can still use Free File Fillable Forms.

H&R Block is a tax preparation company offering online and in-person services for individuals and businesses. H&R Block's online software guides users step-by-step through the filing process, offering explanations and tips along the way. The software also includes audit support and accuracy guarantees, giving filers peace of mind. For those who prefer face-to-face assistance, H&R Block operates thousands of physical locations nationwide where filers can meet with tax professionals in person. H&R Block is a solid choice for filers who want the reassurance of working with a trusted brand and having access to in-person support.

TaxSlayer is a web-based tax preparation software that offers four different pricing plans ranging from basic to premium. Its interface is simple and intuitive, guiding filers through the process with clear instructions and prompts. TaxSlayer offers a wide range of forms and schedules, making it suitable for complex returns, and includes features such as max refund guarantees, priority customer support, and audit defense. TaxSlayer is a cost-effective option for filers who don't require handholding throughout the process and appreciate straightforward pricing structures.

TurboTax is perhaps the most well-known brand in tax preparation software, thanks to its extensive marketing campaigns and long history in the industry. TurboTax offers a range of products for individual and business filers, from free federal filing for simple returns to premium packages for self-employed and corporate filers. TurboTax's software is highly interactive, featuring helpful videos and animations that explain complicated concepts in plain language. The software also integrates with third-party apps and services, making it easier for filers to import data and complete their taxes more efficiently. TurboTax is ideal for filers who want a polished, engaging user experience and advanced features such as integration with outside apps and services.

Coupon Sites

RetailMeNot is one of the most popular coupon sites in the US, with over 700,000 coupons and promo codes available for thousands of stores. They also have a browser extension that alerts you to potential savings while you shop online.

Coupons.com offers digital coupons that can be used at grocery stores, drugstores, and other retailers. Printable coupons, coupon codes, and discounts are also available on their website.

Groupon offers local deals, travel deals, and products at discounted prices. They also have a section dedicated to coupons and promo codes for various merchants.

LivingSocial offers local deals, travel deals, and products at discounted prices. They also have a section for coupons and promo codes.

CouponCabin has been around since 2003 and offers various coupons and promo codes for online shopping. They also offer cashback rebates and have a rewards program for frequent shoppers.

Savings.com offers coupons, promo codes, and deals for thousands of stores. They also have a "Deal of the Day" feature highlighting the best deals they've found daily.

Honey automatically applies coupons and promo codes at checkout when you shop through their platform. They also offer cashback rebates and have a rewards program.

Ebates offers cashback rebates for shopping through their platform. They also have exclusive coupons and promo codes for specific merchants.

TopCashback offers cashback for shopping through their platform, exclusive coupons, and promo codes.

BeFrugal offers coupons, promo codes, and cashback rebates for thousands of stores. They also have a browser extension that alerts you to potential savings while you shop online.

Cost of Living Calculators

Cost of living calculators highlight and consider various key necessities and expenses. Review these sites for more information.

- Numbeo.com
- Livingcost.org
- NerdWallet.com/cost-of-living-calculator

Chapter 12
FROM PAYCHECK TO PROSPERITY

As we close this journey through financial literacy, budgeting, income, responsible spending, debt elimination, saving strategies, and the transformative power of mindset, it's evident that mastering personal finance is both an art and a science. This book has equipped you with the tools and knowledge to navigate today's financial challenges and prepared you to anticipate and adapt to the economic uncertainties of tomorrow.

Financial literacy lays the groundwork for informed decision-making, enabling you to understand and leverage financial concepts. By embracing budgeting, you've learned to direct your financial resources with intention, ensuring that every dollar serves a purpose toward achieving your personal and financial ambitions.

The path toward eliminating debt and saving for the future has underscored the importance of discipline and foresight in financial planning. These chapters have shown that freedom from debt and economic security are achievable with the right strategy and mindset.

The money-saving tips in the book are your arsenal for combating unnecessary expenditures and optimizing your financial resources. They serve as a reminder that small, consistent actions can lead to significant financial gains over time.

Increasing your income encourages self-improvement and opportunity exploration, highlighting that financial growth is about managing what you have and expanding your financial capabilities. Spending responsibly has taught you the value of mindful consumption, ensuring that your spending habits reflect your values and long-term aspirations.

Adopting a positive financial mindset is perhaps the most transformative aspect of this book. It can change how you manage money and view wealth and success. This shift in perspective is crucial for overcoming barriers and fostering a life of abundance.

The exploration of financial tools has demonstrated that in the digital age, managing your finances can be streamlined and even automated, allowing you to focus more on your goals and less on the minutiae of financial management.

As you move forward, remember that personal finance is a continuous learning, adapting, and growing journey. The principles and strategies outlined in this book are not just steps toward financial stability but are the foundation for a life of economic empowerment and independence. Let this book be a compass that guides you through your financial decisions, a beacon of knowledge that lights your way in dark times, and a source of inspiration to pursue your dreams with financial confidence.

Your steps to financial mastery don't end here—it's just beginning. As you turn the final page of this book, you're not closing a chapter on your financial education but stepping into a world of possibilities with the tools, knowledge, and mindset to create a prosperous and fulfilling future. Financial freedom awaits you.

www.ingramcontent.com/pod-product-compliance
Lightning Source LLC
Chambersburg PA
CBHW071057240526
45471CB00016B/1977